W9-ANA-619

795

Portraits of Vision

Portraits of Vision

TOMMY BARNETT

with *SARAH COLEMAN*

THOMAS NELSON PUBLISHERS

NASHVILLE

I dedicate these "Portraits of Vision" to

My father, Reverend Hershel Barnett, who first engraved the love of souls on my heart;

My mother, Joy Barnett, who is everything her name signifies;

My wife, Marja, who has loved and nourished me and given me freedom;

Kristie, Luke, and Matthew, my source of constant pleasure and blessing;

My church staff and board, who have allowed me the freedom to fail—although only once on the same project;

The people of Phoenix First Assembly, whose love and commitment are cherished

You represent the greatest circle of caring
a pastor could ever envision.

Contents

Foreword

TOMMY BARNETT is a one-man journey of love for the Lord. He is also the Arnold Schwarzenegger of the Christian world! He is loving and tough, caring and firm. What you see is what you get. There is nothing false about him. From firsthand experience, I know he is totally refreshing in a world of facade and inconsistency, and he exudes positive influence in lives.

His affectionate and dynamic encouragement encircles a wide body of believers. Because of this, I felt compelled to advocate writing the story of this man and his personal background and explosive ministry—a book relevant to all people and denominations. Many agreed with my premise.

Dr. Pat Robertson, chairman of the board and chief executive officer of The Christian Broadcasting Network, Inc., writes: "To see Phoenix First Assembly is to see a vision become a reality. I can think of no congregation in America as vibrant and as dynamic. Tommy Barnett is truly an inspired man of God who is a pacesetter for all evangelical Christians. *Portraits of Vision* is a blueprint of a concept inspired by the Holy Spirit in the heart of this pastor for building great churches to the glory of almighty God. Few men of God are any more qualified to give to all of us God's vision for the future."

Another perspective comes from Dr. Bill Bright, founder and president of Campus Crusade for Christ, who says, "Tommy Barnett is one of God's great visionaries who has a magnificent view of his Creator and Lord as a God of love and a God of power. Like Jonathan of old, his God can do anything (see 1 Sam. 14:6). Tommy also has a vision for liberating those who live in the darkness and gloom of Satan's kingdom into the glorious kingdom of light—through faithfully proclaiming the 'Light of the world.' I thank God for this man and his faithful, fruitful witness for our dear Savior."

A broad spectrum of lives have been influenced by my pastor, Tommy Barnett. Bob Lilly, legendary Dallas Cowboy, expresses his heart: "Tommy Barnett's love, high energy, and visionary ideas have been a model to Christian athletes in all areas of sports. He has implemented programs for our youth with enthusiasm and gifted organization. He lives out the gospel message. Like a deeply respected coach, he cheers, corrects, and inspires us, willingly and tirelessly, from the sidelines. His walk validates his talk. He is my dear friend and brother in Christ."

A different scope of observation is written by this book's co-author, Sarah Coleman. Brought in by the publisher, her religious tradition and background are different. She shares her research after six months of close scrutiny and investigative search to enrich this project. She says, "I have been involved with books for more than a half century—reading, absorbing everything from the Puritans to ultracontemporary authors. I have personally published, written, ghost-authored, and edited many manuscripts. Working with Tommy Barnett, his staff, family, and people turned a new page in my perception of vision and a true visionary.

"To find a put-down on this pastor, one must go to the man himself. He is unaffected. He uses the dynamic of the Holy Spirit's enabling power to produce change in people and programs. He ignites hidden potential. More than five thousand of his members serve in specific service. He appreciates the skills and ability of women and champions their insight and contribution.

"There will always be those who question the emphasis on numbers, his consuming passion for the less fortunate, and a series of supposed cliches used to motivate pastors and members. Ever present also is the human quest for a chink in the armor of highly visible personalities. To these Tommy Barnett relates, 'We count people because people count. Christ cared about the dispossessed and hurting. Through personal devotion I equip myself with "the whole armor of God." '

"It is clear to me his armor is intact. His 'sword of the Spirit' is not used to injure or hurt. He wears the 'shoes of peace' with dignity and humility.

"These value judgments come from those who know him best and have worked by his side. His life-style does not indicate a rigid, authoritative stance, but the fruit of expected obedience to Jesus Christ.

"*Portraits of Vision* is his story—validated and open-ended—for daily he looks further into the distances of God through the Word and his cherished Selah time."

William Tatham, Jr., is a real estate developer and consultant to Pastor Barnett, and is my EPIC advisory committee colleague. A man strongly involved in the vision and financial accountability of the church, he writes: "Many Christian leaders today profess to receive visions from heaven, but receiving a vision is only half the battle. Pastor Barnett understands that a vision without the proper focus will remain blurred and unfulfilled. His vision of someday pastoring one of the largest Spirit-filled churches in America was not attained by focusing on achieving the vision itself. Instead, our church focus is where it should be: on saving souls for Jesus. This is an example of the type of man necessary to build God's church in today's society—loving but tough, forgiving but uncompromising, humble but aggressive for the Lord. Tommy Barnett is a man who, no matter how bright the vision, keeps his eyes and heart focused on Jesus. He is my best friend on earth."

As a communications consultant, I am aware of the growing variety of ways vision is presented today. At times it is scattered or hyped through media experts, but not by my pastor Tommy Barnett. He has chosen *the* Trilogy, too often disregarded in Christendom: love for the father, fellowship with His Son, and leadership through the person of the Holy Spirit.

Phoenix First Assembly operates in challenge. We are destined to grow and prosper with the undaunted goal of winning souls, healing hurts, and meeting needs. Our prayer for this book is that others will join with us, shoulder to shoulder, to lift high the cross and move forward and onward with greater desire to love Jesus Christ and accept His mandate to share the life-changing message of salvation.

Michael Clifford
President and Founder
Victory Communications
Phoenix, Arizona

Acknowledgments

GRATEFUL ACKNOWLEDGMENT is given to the many contributors, known and unknown, who have helped shape my life and ministry.

A plethora of people have encouraged me through their commitment and commentaries, through their examples and exegesis. Great writers of the past and present find their way into my sermons. My library is blessed with tapes and books that have provided insights—meaningful beyond words.

I am a student of the past. G. Campbell Morgan, William Booth, Charles Finney, Charles Haddon Spurgeon, A. W. Tozer, and George Mueller impact me today. My contemporaries like Dr. Jack Hyles and Dr. Bill Bright provide standards of excellence in developing concepts and programs that have been mine to follow.

Most of all, I acknowledge my father. He was a gregarious individual with an infectious life-style who presented God to Kansas City. He was an innovator of programs and started the first Sunday school bus routes almost half a century ago. His imprint is on my life. He impacted the lives of hundreds of others who now "fly the flag of the gospel" high in their lives and communities. I say it often, Dad was my best encourager!

I acknowledge those individuals who have written books and given me suggestions and thoughts for this book. Some of that appreciated research is included in these pages. I would like to add a special thanks to Douglas Brendel.

I want to acknowledge a pastor's desire to reemphasize statements, phrases, experiences, and philosophies that recur within these pages. We all learn by repetition, and these truths in my heart are commands, not options.

I am especially indebted to Thomas Nelson, Inc., for allowing me a published platform to share my vision with those who are open to winning souls, meeting needs, and healing hurts. A return to the New Testament church is urgently needed as we travel toward the twenty-first century.

Thank you!

*"Where there is no vision,
the people perish."*
—Proverbs 29:18 KJV

*"Where there are no people,
the vision perishes."*
—Tommy Barnett

Introduction

BOOKS HAVE BEEN a continuing source of my education and inspiration. Books are my friends—authored by men and women of yesterday as well as today. The most engaging power of an author is to make new things familiar and familiar things new. The heart and substance of this book is to accomplish that mission.

The statement is as old as antiquity, recorded in God's Book: "Where there is no vision, the people perish." An old truth made new: "Where there are no people, the vision perishes" is the reason I believe people count and so we count people.

My vision began as a sixteen-year-old evangelist. It grew during an evangelistic career that took me many times around the world. Maturity showed me that *vision* in the hands of God experiences *re-vision*. I learned that evangelism was not the only key that brought people to Christ. Winning souls unlocked the door to church growth. Revision of thinking showed me I could never lead by intimidation. Inspiration was the pattern of Christ—and people would follow me if I followed the Lord.

The unmistakable *pro-vision* for me as an individual, and for our family and ministries has been heaven designed. Jesus is my source, my resource, and my goal. I learned that within the house of God, with seventy-six members, a pastor has the resource and people to move to five hundred and from five hundred to one thousand. I have experienced the many faces of provision and find them emerging from the very rich and extremely poor—although neither source was "poor in spirit."

Writing this book with Sarah Coleman, who shares many of the same heroes, allowed an emphasis on the magnificent truth of the Holy Spirit as a person, not an experience. That thought is contrary to natural expectations. As a pastor and teacher of soul-winning, need-meeting, hurt-healing philosophy, I am not led by the natural, but the supernatural—the *super-vision* of the Holy Spirit.

We present *Portraits of Vision* within a jacket of prayer. My platform for the chapters has been the pulpit, as well as my everyday life. I am the product of homegrown love—love across many generations of ministry. I am an open book, and many of the pages of my life and ministry are written herein, including the wonderful victories, while acknowledging the failures.

My ultimate source is God, through Jesus Christ and the person of the Holy Spirit—indeed the holy men of God—authors of life and eternal life, who daily make "old things familiar and familiar things new!"

Tommy Barnett
Phoenix, Arizona

PART ONE

Vision

1

The Vision That Gets God's Attention

THE PARADE OF MINISTRIES was about to begin. The familiar Olympic Game theme of champions played in the background. Enthusiastic celebrants were in place with colorful banners. Cross-cultural children, men and women from the streets, musicians, people in wheelchairs, pregnant young girls, the wealthy and the poor, were all lined up together—their common denominator their love of Jesus. They were living pictures of Psalm 111:1, "I will celebrate the Lord with my whole heart."

This parade represented a hundred ministries, and more than a thousand points of light! Its leadership and work force came from nearly five thousand committed volunteers who worked and worshiped together at Phoenix First Assembly. As their pastor, I stood to the right of center stage, and I humbly began the evening's service, kicking off the annual Pastors' Conference with my personal vision of how to get God's attention.

I told the story of when Jesus came into a city. Everybody in that city was excited, which was not an abnormal reaction in His early ministry. For when Jesus came, multitudes followed because every place He went, the Bible affirms, He went about doing good. The throngs met

Him. The lame, the halt, the diseased, the children—all jockeyed to get His attention.

For some who were handicapped or weak, getting His attention was almost impossible. Yet one woman, so sickly that she could hardly get there, pressed her way into the crowd. For twelve years she "had suffered many things from many physicians. She had spent all that she had and was no better, but rather grew worse" (Mark 5:26). Luke, an evangelist and physician, admitted she could not be healed (Luke 8:43); she had been given a terminal diagnosis.

Disheartened and discouraged, she managed to brush the hem of Jesus' garment. She was pierced with fear when she heard Him ask His disciples, "Who touched me?"

In amazement they responded that with the throngs of people present, they could hardly know who had touched Him.

Gazing out over the Parade of Ministries, I underlined this observation: "Among the crowd and obvious confusion, a dying woman got Jesus' attention. She did something that attracted Him. I want to know how to get the attention of God. What did that woman do to focus the attention of God—that caused Jesus to stop and look?"

I went on to explain that many years ago, I left a pastorate in Davenport, Iowa, where I had served for eight and one-half years, and came to Phoenix. It was difficult to know what to expect in this fast-growing city of sun and cactus. I was tired in body and in spirit. I had confessed to God that I would never pastor a church again.

Davenport had been a challenge. I had felt the call of God there when there were only seventy-six people in my pastorate—but I left a burgeoning church. Building that church had taken its toll. Now I was about to pastor again, from a call of God and a congregation numbering about two hundred on Sundays. A church that in the past had run over one thousand. Thoughts of why that change in numbers tumbled in my head. These were good people with good programs. They had a fine choir and children's choices—all the accouterments to success, and yet they were losing people. There had been no revival.

I believe the Bible when it defines the New Testament church, which had people "added daily to the church." I looked at the ministerial crowd gathered below me and said, "Inquiring minds often ask me the same question. They want to know if there is anything wrong with a small church. My answer never changes. No—not for a week! For if you have a New Testament church, *you cannot stay small!* The church grows daily and weekly. God pours out His blessings when your vision gets His attention. The Bible is clear: 'Where there is no vision, the people perish' (Prov. 29:18 KJV). The logic is self-evident that *where there are no people, the vision perishes.*

One day I started driving around Phoenix, and I began to examine what other churches were doing to reach the city. I had come from a town where we ran forty buses and reached thousands of kids. It was expensive and at times mind-boggling. I wasn't sure I could do it again. But as I surveyed these churches, many of them outstanding in their leadership and programs, I realized that few were reaching or focusing on the inner city.

I went back to my new board and told them that we were surrounded by ghettos, multiples of need, numerous children—and it appeared they had no church. I challenged them in that meeting to reach these people for the glory of God. I asked if they would buy me four buses.

It was very quiet in the boardroom. Then came the questions that pastors are all too familiar with. What does it cost? Could we wait until we have a few more people? What about launching that program *after* we build the new church?

Knowing from past experience that there is never a "good time" and seldom "enough money," I reminded them of their agreement when I came not to discourage my vision. After deliberation, they bought me four buses. The first Sunday we ran them, they were filled. I went back a month later and asked the same board for ten more buses. They gulped, but they bought me ten more. A bit more than a month later, I got ten more and they were filled. The next time I asked, they responded in chorus: "Praise God!" As time went by, Phoenix First Assembly learned new ways to use those buses and to multiply their effectiveness for more than Sunday transportation. The buses provided the route to growth, and incredible growth ensued.

It is not surprising that the New Testament concept still is a model. Christ was moved with compassion by the multitude. He fed the *five thousand* and came to seek and to save *all* who are lost. *Winning souls, healing hurts, meeting needs* through *loving people* and *believing in people* is a biblical profile of growth.

Suddenly Phoenix First Assembly was bringing in a different crowd. Not a better crowd, a different crowd. This concerned one of the families who had been longtime members. "This church is going to ruin," said one to another, "with all these inner-city urchins. We are worried about our safety." The next Sunday was Easter. One of the hymns was "Man of Sorrows, What a Name." The first verse spoke to that specific family in vivid impression.

> "Man of Sorrows," what a name
> For the Son of God who came
> Ruined sinners to reclaim. Hallelujah!
> What a Saviour.
> —P. P. Bliss

The family "caught" a different vision. They became participants in my vision. People were learning what God does with "ruined things." God exchanges "beauty for ashes." God is in the reclamation business. The message was coming across. There would be no "disposable people" in this church. We all need reminding that the greatest *ruin* of all was Calvary. The price of redemption was ugly. But as the Puritans used to say, "God took Calvary's nightmare and transformed it into the cradle of salvation." The stone was rolled away from that empty tomb, not to let Jesus out, but to let us look in and know that "I AM" of the "I am the resurrection and the life" as a person—one to meet and to transform each life and make it whole.

Kids flocked to Phoenix First Assembly from the housing projects and other underprivileged areas. Members got excited about being involved. Last Good Friday weekend, thirty-three thousand youngsters in several football fields across town had an Easter Egg Hunt. Those stadiums were flooded with kids and parents, and literally thousands received Christ and were followed up under the direction of Mark Lampley. (The church census that weekend exceeded fifty thousand!)

Through the running of the buses, Phoenix First Assembly began to explode. Things were happening—when you have God's attention, you learn to go with the flow, and to praise God from whom all blessings flow!

The orchestra picked up the beat, and hundreds of little bus kids stepped off the Parade of Ministries. I was as excited as the children. They sang at the top of their lungs. I interviewed several of them. Some kids had no known parents. Rarely did one parent ever come to church. One kid wanted to be a preacher. Others nodded their assent. Scripture verses flowed out from them, and it was difficult not to let them steal the rest of the show.

But the parade must go on! More people came up on stage—people who had been discovered through the bus kids. These are a host of hurting men and women who needed special attention. There were those who didn't know how to act in church, and some who had never heard the name Jesus. The educably slow passed by grinning from ear to ear. Faces reflected the love and care of the people who were pouring the love of Jesus into them, sometimes with response, sometimes with no response. But they still "poured."

The Son-Beams sang a song using posters and hand signals. All arms and all legs mixed with slow motion were the punctuation marks of their song, and the audience was moved to tears. One Son-Beam prayed a simple prayer for "my pastor, who is always full of hugs, with love and tenderness in abundance for his people." It was a warm, loving prayer that got the attention of God.

Another way to get God's attention is a vision for the blind and crippled. "The blind receive sight and the lame walk, the lepers are cleansed and the deaf hear, and the dead are raised up, and the poor have the gospel preached to them" (Matt. 11:5 NAS). Just as the blind man was carried out to the Gate beautiful and healed, so these people needed to be carried into God's house for the work that awaited being accomplished in their lives.

Ola is blind and deaf. As a minority woman she grew up with her share of obstacles. Now she loves God. She had prepared a song for the parade, explained through the interpreter, busy translating on this woman's fingers. Ola sang "Jesus Loves Me" in an unsteady monotone—the kind that surely caused the angels to sing their response back into Ola's heart.

The church's Holy Rollers come onto the stage. These are wheelchair-ished individuals led by Sharon Henning. The orchestra picked up again. The conference pastors cheered.

Piloted by the love of members who are involved with these people, church is their haven of hope and greatest source of joy.

One of the Holy Rollers, handicapped from birth, said it appeared that the churches she had been in, prior to this one, had "everything for the churches, but nothing for the crippled people."

The parade came to another halt. As God's "big wheels" moved off, one was detained. His name is Randy. Randy had been beaten and left to die on the streets. No one ever found out by whom or why. He was not able to talk or walk, and when he came out of a coma at the county hospital, the doctors said he would be a vegetable for life. Now, through the love of the Wheelchair Ministry, Randy is learning to walk—at times he walks without a cane. Volunteers are working with him, using index cards, and he is starting to make sounds and talk. Bus pastors, assistants and their workers vie with each other for the privilege of taking Randy home with them for special visits. He is a joy. He wears the physical and emotional scars of the past, but is becoming one of God's brilliant stars. (As this book goes to press, Randy is walking and talking.)

Literacy specialists may say people's memory declines with the years. However, many of these people learn a new verse every week. Their minds are being healed. All too frequently starting with a drooping head and dry mouth, they graduate to a head held high and a mouth that speaks of the love of Jesus. A ninety-five-year-old regular attender boasts of eating seven pieces of fried chicken at a wheelchair special event. It was verified. Another longs to be a sports mascot. The congregation seeks people to take these loved ones to games and events as part of the family. A wonderful way to spill love all over ones who have been deprived of hope for so long.

Back at the parade, the pastor tells of a Thanksgiving dinner shared with one of the couples, an event stored in the memory bank of these people for many years to come.

Marching on stage in uniform and with musical precision came representatives of the Spanish Ministry. This mariachi group of clarion trumpets and magnificent strings presented a celebration of their culture and their love of God. Recently Phoenix First Assembly installed earphones for translation—designed to reach more people whose barrier to Jesus is simply language.

From my place on stage, I found myself longing for the thousands of pastors in attendance not to look at the Parade of Ministries as a "pastoral show" but as a demonstration of what focuses God's attention. I prayed they were receiving the message that in getting God's attention, you did not have to look far. *Just everywhere!*

This is a world where there are lots of new hurts taking place—things that are easy to push aside, things that are hidden in closets. Because of this, the Phoenix church has formed a political action group.

Their leader, an attorney's wife, articulately spoke to the crowd about issues faced today involving the church. She reminded the pastors from around the country that pornography is an eight billion dollar industry. She spoke of Ted Bundy, pointing out that his crimes began with pornography, even the *Playboy* magazines in the grocery stores. In addition, the facts were evident that schools were buffeting young people with the knowledge that 10 percent could be homosexual, and counseling them on how to accept it—and then there were the cries of the unborn—all issues needing the attention of God's people. She reminded the crowd that "where sin abounds, grace does much more abound," and pleaded that churches get involved. If churches were too timid to speak out, they were agreeing with what was going on, yielding their influence to the enemy. Each of us has a role to fulfill. The Puritans said, *"When you pray, move your feet"*.

Following her speech the banners paraded by, calling attention to the Overcomers from Alcohol, a support group within the church. They were followed by His Sheltering Wing, born in the hearts of a couple who provided a home with a Christian atmosphere, where they could teach the word and help young expectant mothers make abortion alternative decisions. Soon the house next door opened up, and they rented it for others.

As the girls walked by, some very pregnant, some with babies in their arms, a softness settled on the audience. This was another example of faith at work, of my belief that *the past has no future*.

One of the girls spoke. She was radiant as she shared her story. Before coming to His Sheltering Wing she had no direction and no future. She had come from a good family, but things went wrong. When she learned she was pregnant, she was on her own with no money. The Gene Johnsons pointed her to Christ. She was taught how to care for her child, after making a thorough investigation as to her alternatives. In giving everything to the Lord—her life and little boy—things started to happen. She went through college, got a wonderful job. Now, only twenty years old, she has her own home, a car, and tithes—with plenty left over to care for her and the child. She related that she never takes anything for granted, especially the love of God that was shed on her through those who took her in and demonstrated "a better way."

I smiled softly at the girl, then grew serious again as I related, "The church is reaching out, but we can still do better." The people who were passing by were the center of God's love and must be a large part of the love all of us have to give. Probably one of the most difficult and sensitive issues for the church today is AIDS. The AIDS Ministry people stopped at the podium to bring a new awareness of this killer.

God called a wonderful couple, somewhat new to Phoenix First Assembly, to head this priority ministry. This was another case of finding a need and filling it—of seeing a hurt and working to heal it.

Leo Godzich, a brilliant young man, was sitting in the balcony with his wife at a Pastors' School one year and heard me say that sometime soon this church would be ministering to people who were really hurting. At that moment, Leo saw a vision of himself hugging a skinny little AIDS victim, and in the background he saw his family coming to the Lord on their knees. It was a shocking and disquieting experience. He went on to explain that when he was in the world he had no time for people with an aberrant life-style—none for the homosexual—and was one of the first to be free with AIDS jokes. Then Jesus spoke to him through His words: "Verily I say unto you, Inasmuch as ye have done it unto one of the least of these my brethren, *ye have done it unto me*" (Matt. 25:40, emphasis added).

"Wherefore, I put thee in remembrance that thou stir up the gift of God, which is in thee by the putting on of my hands. For God hath not given us the spirit of fear; but of power, and of love, and of a sound mind" (2 Tim. 1:6–7).

The AIDS Ministry is "kindling afresh that gift of God," thus allowing God who gives us those good gifts to return those gifts back to Him for His glory.

AIDS people tend to hide when they come to the dying stage of their illness. One came to this church. How? Very reluctantly. He had been turned away from other places of worship—asked outright by ministers to leave. He was fragile, but came to a strong realization of who Christ is. How did he die? Victorious in Christ. Eternal triumph in the midst of tragedy. The broken, physical deterioration of these people who have no control of bodily functions is pathetic to see. Yet, when one comes to faith, and is certain of where eternity will be spent, an infusion of joy and peace settles on that disintegrating body, producing a healthy soul headed for wholeness.

Every congregation will be or is now affected. The Centers for Disease Control states that one out of every twenty-three men between the ages of twenty-one and fifty-one in the United States is an AIDS carrier. More Americans have died from AIDS than perished in Vietnam. Unfortunately, the media has desensitized the public to the intensity of this need. When the church, by action, admits the lack of a coping process, it is unconscionable. *God calls us not just to cope, but to conquer.* "But in all these things we overwhelmingly conquer through Him who loved us" (Rom. 8:37 NAS).

Is there hope when it comes to AIDS? In 1988 a brother who had been diagnosed as AIDS-HIV-positive was saved from a life-style of homosexuality. He had serious AIDS symptoms when he began looking for a church for support and found what the other patient had experienced—churches were not receptive to him. Even though he was constantly rejected, he never lost faith in God. Leo met with him and ministered to him. Months later he went back to the hospital for an unrelated illness, and at that time they took blood tests. Looking at the results, the doctors became confused. They took more tests. They could not explain what was going on in his body. Not only had the AIDS virus disappeared, his T-cell blood count was above normal, which had never happened.

This man was introduced to the pastors. The parade of ministries had taken an incredible turn. Someone diagnosed as "hopeless" was recovering. The former AIDS patient shared his story. He explained how grateful he was to be a witness to the church of a living miracle to honor the Lord Jesus Christ. He explained that he was simply an ambassador for Christ, who snatched him from the jaws of hell. As an outcast and a sinner, laden with faults, God saw him as complete and whole through Jesus.

He is going around to places that are open to him, knocking on doors where there is need, and sharing what God can do. He is asking the church to catch a new glimpse of needs; to be able to see with the eyes of Jesus, and with the heart and compassion of Jesus, and the mind of Christ. It is truly then the church experiences the reality of what Paul discussed in 1 Corinthians 6:9–11.

The AIDS Ministry continues at Phoenix First Assembly. It is a ministry that gets God's attention through ministering to "the least of these" and in so doing, they are ministering to Him.

The Parade of Ministries moved ahead with the Saturday Soul-Winning Society, the Prison Ministries, walking by in chains and striped suits. Next came men who carried the cross and preached in the streets. Then there were the walkie-talkie preachers, coffee house preachers, Sunday school and Women's Ministries, and Park Ministries. At the Park Ministries, the procession stopped again. Here were people with stories as individual as their own signatures. Their stories were different, but each carried a common thread—addictions, loss of family, sin, and hopelessness.

VISIONS ARE CAUGHT, NOT TAUGHT

Eight years ago the church fed six thousand on a special Sunday for people who came to church. The next time they fed fifteen thousand. At this event Richard Bomar "caught" a vision of those in need. He felt it was one thing to feed the people from the street, but quite another to see them restored. Richard bought a mobile home and started putting homeless men inside, telling them about God, and helping them find jobs. He bought another house trailer and another. Then he bought a house and finally an apartment that is crowded with men, and now women and families in need. His staff goes out and recruits street people, and when they come to the Lord Jesus Christ, they are true trophies of grace.

Asked what motivated him to work, Richard Bomar said to the crowd in all humility that "Our duty to God is to do all we can, or we are unprofitable servants. We are just doing our duty. God broke me with His love and I love Him and others. These men can be miracles. Those in this Parade of Ministries, from the street, are already miracles! God takes the bits and pieces of men that have been spread from one end of the continent to the other and puts them back together and here they stand tonight. God is in the business of picking up the broken pieces and healing the wounds in our lives. Old things *do* pass away; all things are new."

Victor testified of twenty months and eighteen hundred miles before getting to where God could deal with him. He was lost and a prisoner of his aloneness. Tired and ashamed, he saw a white bus go by and said that someday he would catch that bus and come to Phoenix First Assembly. He did, was saved, and then went to Park Ministries. Because he was fearful of looking for a job, the director allowed him to stay at the house for three and one-half months. He read the Word, was built up, and then was ready to act on God's Word, realizing that God and His Word are one. "God was with him."

Today Victor is head custodian at the church and goes around singing, "Jesus got into my heart and into my soul. I used to be oh, so sad, But now I'm oh, so glad. Jesus got a hold of my life and He won't let me go!"

Another street person salvaged by the grace of God was Richard Hudulla. Saved for only a year, he came from another state, broken and full of destructive habits. He had owned a business with many employees, a fine home, family, a Mercedes and more. In his distress, Richard was loved and sought after by the Park Ministries, and one day his life changed.

Richard is an outstanding accountant and business person. He carries a heavy load, managing this ministry and doing other work for the church. Said Richard, "I can't imagine that anyone would want to reach down and pick up a guy out of the muck and mire, dead in sins and trespasses, dying from alcoholism, and deliver him. Give him a new heart, completely heal and restore him. But that's what Jesus is all about!"

The Parade of Ministries took on a more dignified air as the deacon board representatives came by, followed by the EPIC (Executive Planning and Information Committee). Blue-ribbon individuals who work for God, many have built great corporations. Their acumen is a necessity in a church and facility as large and far-reaching as Phoenix First Assembly.

The EPIC is new and is comprised of businesspersons who help reach the city. These individuals of means and power have chosen Phoenix First Assembly not because they have been wooed but because they have seen results. They come because they invest in people. They see bottom-line return on their investments. They appreciate and maintain integrity, and feel privileged to be in this work of God, which strives to carry out the biblical mandate to "heal hurts, meet needs, and care for the poor."

The parade continued passing by: a children's choir, Wills and

Trusts, Early Childhood Ministry, Deaf Ministry, Children's Church, Visitation, Preaching and Interpreting, Family Ministries, volunteer pastors—those between pulpits who donated their time and experience and who often come to be encouraged.

Next came Brother Alvin Booher, eighty-six years old. Last year, he prayed with seven thousand patients in hospitals, and more than fifteen-hundred received Christ.

As pastor, I have the cards to prove it and they were all followed up.

The Fashion Share Luncheon passed by. They hosted a magnificent event, inviting park, street, and bus mothers to come downtown for a wonderful luncheon. They provided appropriate clothes for the women, and then give them the opportunity to be clothed in His garment of righteousness. Bringing up the rear of the Parade of Ministries was the Athletes Ministry, led by Larry Kerychuk. Pro athletes and Hall of Famers were with him—men who would stand and say Jesus is Lord—women who were making a difference in competition because of Christ.

Illustrated Sermons passed by, with Video Services—animals and actors representing productions, along with highly skilled audio and video technicians.

I paused to greet a new ministry to Mormons—seventy-eight were at their first meeting. Joyfully, I asked the people to validate this new challenge by "saying a good amen!" *They did!*

The Twenty-Four-Hour Crisis Line, telephone in hand, was represented. The stories of suicides averted and people blessed and helped and rescued are constant on-line events. The Watchmen, directed by Jack Wallace, oversee three hundred square miles of Phoenix, so if there is a neighborhood need, there is a Watchman to respond to that need immediately.

The end, but really a new beginning for several dozen young people, is the Master's Commission. A solid-year program of prayer, Bible study and memorization, discipline, and constant ministry is the heartbeat of its pastor, Lloyd Zieglar. Some of the students came from bus routes. The alumni are scattered around the country and world, reproducing what they have learned. What have they learned? To make every day a Master-piece.

The Parade of Ministries ends. The banners come down. The buses load the kids, the wheelchair buses secure the Holy Rollers. The guest pastors react teary-eyed and spiritually moved. Together, they all have *celebrated a vision* this particular night—*a portrait of vision that gains the attention of God!*

2

The Visionary

VISIONARIES ACT!

Academics study!

When the two are interfaced, a new portrait of innovation is discovered. My personal vision is clear. It comes from an awareness of my spiritual destiny and an intensive library that includes classics—tapes and volumes and study books. I believe in visions, dreams, and goals—as long as those are God's goals, God's dreams, and God's visions. If they are in the plan of God, I write them on the tablet of my heart, and then test to assure they will glorify God. If convinced, I go for them with zeal, with conviction and confidence that "He who has begun a good work in you will perform it until the day of Jesus Christ" (Phil. 1:6).

I am steadfast in my belief that "In the beginning God created," and the Creator has a specific plan which has already preceded Him. The Creator prepares the way with divine dimension. To illustrate this, recall when Jesus was heading for the cross. The Master sent His people ahead to prepare the way for His entrance into the city. He told them He wanted them to go to a very specific place. There they would locate a man with a donkey. He would take them to a designated house. Everything was planned for His life.

God has so ordered our lives that not only preordained dreams and visions exist, but the plan is in place. The fulfillment of a dream, goal, or vision that is in synchronization with God's eternal plan succeeds. Even the budget is not a primary issue! Therefore the man of God moves forward in the Spirit of the Lord and in the will of God, knowing that whatever comes across his path, he will deal with, because God has a plan. Jesus' life was a life of "following out" what the Father was doing. It is a wonderful life to follow out what the Father has for a Christian to do.

I will never stop dreaming, but within those parameters there are certain things that I know for sure—and am convinced of through the Spirit of God—which are constants and not changeable. These four things I *know* and believe God has implanted in my heart, and the "visionary" part of my being operates within these established lines.

1. I *know* I am called to pastor this church. It is to be a pattern of good works and an example for others to see my God-given vision of a New Testament church. I want to inspire others to do the work of the ministry.

2. I *know* I have been called to reach out to people and to challenge them as to what God can do with their lives. I have many times observed that God uses *the ordinary to accomplish the awesome*.

3. I *know* I am to make tapes, write books, and provide video materials to encourage and enrich the body of Christ. I want everything I do to lift up the name of the Lord and to glorify God. I want to instill in people that *after you find a peak, the next vision and dream should be a higher one*. With God as your partner, it is assured!

   But as it is written, Eye hath not seen, nor ear heard, neither hath entered into the heart of man, the things which God hath prepared for them that love Him. But God hath revealed them unto us by His Spirit: for the Spirit searcheth all things, yea, the deep things [plans] of God. For what man knoweth the things of a man, save the Spirit of man which is in him? Even so the things of God knoweth no man, but the Spirit of God. (1 Cor. 2:9–11)

4. Another thing I *know* God has called me to is to be in my pulpit on Sundays and Wednesday nights. Only once did I miss a Wednesday night unless I was out of the country or on vacation. Likewise, only a few times have I missed a Sunday service. That

is what God put in my heart. Impressive and alluring invitations have challenged that commitment, but I keep it because I believe it is from God.

As God's people we need to *know* the purpose and goals of our lives. Then the reins of leadership are in the hands of God. Since I was sixteen years old and preaching, I have never wanted for a place to preach. Why? Because God has been in control. Before the foundation of the world, His plan was in place for me. "Before I formed you in the womb I knew you . . . I have appointed you." (Jer. 1:5 NAS).

My vision is "forever settled in heaven," and I have a given-and-found rest in God's preordained plan for me. My dreams and visions are constant companions. I easily understand the heartbeat of visionaries like Dr. Paul Cho, pastor of the mega-church in Korea.

A group of believers had come to Dr. Cho's office in Seoul to see some items that he said God had provided for him. When they found the room barren, they were confused. They asked him where the merchandise was that he had stated God had given to him. Much to their astonishment, Dr. Cho pointed to his heart. "They are here," he said, continuing to touch his left side. "You cannot see them because my spirit inside of me acts as the incubator. Soon they will be birthed. You will see!"

Through the years, Dr. Cho's friends have pointed to his heart and asked with interest how many things are "incubating." Often weeks or months later they become spectators to the accomplished vision.

I carry "visions" in my heart. The Holy Spirit writes the blueprints and the invisible images take brick and mortar, flesh and blood, the shape of a wheelchair bus, an illustrated sermon, or a cause. Should it be surprising to "see things" that are not yet reality? Of course not! The eyes of faith focus with expectation.

> While we look not at the things which are seen, but at the things which are not seen; for the things which are seen are temporal, but the things which are not seen are eternal. (2 Cor. 4:18 NAS)

> If we hope for that we see not, then do we with patience wait for it. (Rom. 8:25)

How are my visions accomplished? *Through people.* I believe in people. I am convinced that people really want to do something of value for

God. I do not accept that people are lazy. There is something inherent in the heart of believers that longs to serve. After offering "the gift of God which is everlasting life," I believe that the greatest gift to be offered to a congregation is *the gift of opportunity!* It is crucial to show them that within everyone is spiritual greatness, and that *mediocrity is unacceptable.*

God's people have to be special. They are invited to have "the mind of Christ." The Holy Spirit, the resident truth teacher, is there so each is endued with supernatural power—power designed for the purposes of God in His prepared people. The people are prepared through consistent teaching on the basics in Christian living. They learn by repetition and attention. *Reaffirming the basics and giving attention to what gets God's attention builds commitment.*

The pressure is taken off the individual who may appear timid at the huge challenge the church presents, by realizing from the staff and pastor that *God is the Creator. God's servant is the doer of His creativity.* This is emphasized over and over. People are channels of the creative power of God. They are simply to carry out what has accomplished before time began. He has the power, we are the conduit of that power. Romans 11:36 NAS supplies a liberating truth: "For from Him and through Him and to Him are all things. To Him be the glory forever." Scripture reminds us that "from Him"—He is the source of all creativity. "Through Him" we are the resource. "To Him" clearly displays that He is the goal of all that we do. That way the glory goes back to Him forever. *Say a good Amen!*

My motivational technique was not learned in a book, although I am an avid reader. I do not move about the church campus as a rigid captain of a tight ship. I try to lead by example, *by inspiration, not intimidation.* A godly motivation encourages and enriches people. When I tell my people they can do it, they believe it. I stand behind them. I show them. When they finally catch a part of a dream of their own, they follow it and fulfill it. That way we all know that God can do everything but fail.

I have built two churches that were voted "the fastest-growing churches in America." I have been called many things, but *noncontroversial* and *predictable* are not among them. You cannot be one to establish workable dynamics of church growth or head a thriving church aflame without a pocket full of surprises.

These must appear with unrelenting regularity!

At Christmas angels fly over the auditorium symbolizing their message of two thousand years ago to "fear not." More than one hundred thousand people attended. At Easter one thousand members of the church participated in bringing the Resurrection story to another throng of visitors. Children delighted in the seven-thousand-pound popsicles—with the hope of getting into the *Guinness Book of World Records*. The same was true of a gigantic iced lollipop. These are means to encourage the youth to participate in events that will share the truest meaning of Easter.

The annual Fourth of July weekend extravaganza, another surprise event, brings upwards of twenty thousand people. It is a red, white, and blue-ribbon spectacular. The American flag is built fifty feet long and thirty-five feet wide. Several hundred people are placed upon it with an orchestra at the base. The event is a combination of a camp meeting and sing-along with fireworks, as planes flying over drop skydivers who land in the field trailing banners exalting "Jesus is Lord." Patriotic songs are intermingled with old gospel songs. At the close, ten thousand balloons with the church logo are released to float across the city. A great musical and stirring message and altar call follow, ending with the "The Battle Hymn of the Republic." Reported one observer:

> When the "Battle Hymn" started and the fireworks shot to the heavens, I wondered if Barnett was orchestrating the booms of the pryomedia display to the drum rolls of the music! Everybody's fur was standing up on their necks and even an old reprobate like me was standing at attention. Not just to salute America, but to God's truth which keeps marching on!

And that it does at this church, set on a hill, carved closely by the Shadow Mountains. An unexpected observation came from a Red Guard member from China. He came to see the Grand Canyon and great places in America. He said, "This church topped it all!"

Other Christian happenings are staged in the church auditorium which seats seven thousand. Illustrated sermons are people-pleasing times. They are not done for entertainment, but to show the story of Christ and the Christian life. Nevertheless, they exhibit the professionalism of docudramas and elaborate productions.

Whatever the future unfolds, Phoenix First Assembly—"the church with a heart"—is staying close to the heart of God. That heart stretches to expanding square miles of need. Although I was forced to move to the northern suburbs of one of the fastest-growing cities in America, Phoenix First Assembly's presence is widely felt.

A body of believers cannot be bound by class or economic distinction. My heart pours into depressed Phoenix more than the areas of affluency. A black church, a white church, a rich church, a poor church—that is not Christianity. You can reach all cultures, races, backgrounds, and economic strata with the gospel. Phoenix First Assembly's philosophy is that every member is a minister. Some ministers fear their congregation. I do not. I preach as if I were preaching to ministers. I train our people to carry out the commands of the Bible in the everyday work of the church. People may criticize our means, but they can't criticize the end. The end is people who are changed. People who have been lost, on whom society has given up, and are now productive human beings. The method isn't sacred, the message is. We use incentives and rewards, not gimmicks. Our emphasis is on the gospel and doing right. Too often critics focus on the few big days and other special events we have, and they ignore the good we do hour by hour, day by day.

The results of the good, "hour by hour and day by day" were proof-positive in a recent parking lot survey, unrehearsed and extemporaneous, on a spring morning at Phoenix First Assembly. Said a man, chronologically around thirty, but looking old and worn: "This church saved my life. It is my safety net, and showed me Jesus. I now am a guy who feels he has had God's scrub brush and a hose reach into my filth and make me as clean as God promised—it now helps me wear God's best robe."

Contrasting was a little girl who had run around the other side of one of the fifty-plus buses. When asked if she knew who Tommy Barnett was, she quickly responded, "Yeah, he's my *pasture*." There was sweet irony in that statement. The "pasture" feeds the sheep and lambs. The youngster quickly pointed out that her other "pasture" was the bus driver!

As the wheelchairs were being unloaded, one woman was asked of the church's significance and responded, "This church? It took me from being 'anesthetized' to being 'magnified' to God. Pretty good, huh?"

The researcher slipped to the background, into the crowd, wondering if this was a person from among the many nursing home people who had been kept suppressed and quiet by medication, feeling no self-worth and just waiting for the inevitable. Her statement was understood. Once she was asleep to the realities of what Browning wrote:

> 'Grow old along with me, The best is yet to be
> The last for which the first is made
> Our times are in His hand who said
> "A whole I planned. Trust God.
> Be not afraid."

She liked waking from that former "sleep" and being given the chance now to magnify the Lord and recapture that lost self-worth. For to be *known*, we have to be *known* of God.

A family piled out of a packed station wagon. The enthusiasm stood out as if they were headed for a Superbowl Sunday. In their hearts, Phoenix First Assembly offered "Superbowl fever" daily. They walked toward the sanctuary with a gait that recorded, "This is a championship event. We are about to score another goal and receive another prize—bringing someone else to Jesus." That was just what they were doing. A new family had moved into Scottsdale, next door. They were introducing them to their church. Even the young children acted like cheerleaders, tugging on the jackets of their new friends and leading them in the right direction—and, prayerfully, up the steps to faith.

A man stepped out of a Porsche. His Brooks Brothers clothes spoke of means. An old truck pulled alongside of him. He greeted the truckload as family. He related that this church had provided the "impact relationship" he sought for in former days of cults, therapy, New-Age books, and events. He described the church and its pastor as "like a giant, wrapped package. You can reach into it after untying the ribbon of God's love, and just keep receiving and receiving and receiving." One day he will start to refill the bounty—so that others may receive.

My vision for the church emerged after sixteen years as an evangelist. It was a blessing to travel the world and share the gospel. *Crusading* is exciting. *Conserving* is another matter. I became increasingly aware that the lost were saved at revivals, camps, and special meetings. I wondered why this was not a common event for the church. After all, the church was God's arm to reach the lost and dying world.

I started a personal search which continues today for soul-winning churches and found few. However, the profile of those churches were ones that were growing. The churches I had grown up with—those of my father—were consistent patterns of growth. My dad may have been the first pastor to go for poor children and introduce buses as a means of reaching the lost. My dad's example was strong. Some of my other early vision was "caught" from a man I have never met, but who has been a continuing influence on my ministry.

From Jack Hyles' examples, I learned that *great works do not just happen. They are caused.*

When moving to Davenport, Iowa, to assume my first pastorate, dad's files and Dr. Hyles's files were much in my mind. Westside would be a soul-winning church. Early on I was able to present souls to my new congregation by saying, "Great churches are soul-winning churches. Our people have a magnificent obsession—and that is to win souls to Jesus Christ." Growth came quickly. After three years at Westside, I asked Johnny Cash to be a guest of the church. The thought of this rally had "incubated" for a long time. Johnny Cash and I had corresponded for some time after Johnny's life was turned around for Christ.

The church pulled together in a massive attempt to prepare a stadium that dismissed a circus only hours before the Cash event. O'Donnell Stadium was set up by members, giving their all, remembering that great works never happen—they are caused! Sixteen thousand people poured into the stadium to hear Johnny Cash sing and share that he cared for people and that Jesus Christ had changed his life. Westside Assembly gained a lot of attention and, more importantly, five thousand people responded to the invitation to receive Jesus Christ.

What are the long-term results of such mass evangelism? Kathy Macoumber and her husband lived in Davenport. They were Johnny Cash fans. When they learned he would be appearing, *free,* they made plans to come. At the invitation they went forward—not to pray, but to take close-ups of their favorite performer.

But God had started a work in their hearts. Being Catholic, Kathy had issues to settle. They returned to Westside Assembly to learn more. Both were saved. Today Kathy is an integral part of the Music Ministry at Phoenix First Assembly. She is a valued asset and a viable conduit in programming and planning. Her husband plays the saxophone. Both thank God for *big events!*

It has been said before, vision is caught, not taught. Jack Hyles, still unknown to me, had imparted a vision that was caught and now is magnified in my life and through our church.

Through that one event, attendance increased about two hundred fifty people per Sunday. "Ask of me and I shall give thee the heathen for thine inheritance and the uttermost parts of the earth for thy possession" (Ps. 2:8).

I am often amazed and astonished at how helpful and willing to work people are if you have a vision and clearly communicate that vision. I look at my own life in the light of who Jesus Christ is, and believe I have a mandate, not just to succeed but to *exceed*. If God provided heaven's best in the person of Jesus Christ, then I feel I must give my personal best back to God. Jesus said, "I am come that they may have life, and that they may have it more abundantly" (John 10:10). Abundant life is found in "wringing the most out of every day," or how to overdose on living! With focus we can learn ways to do this and to reproduce our vision in the lives of others—with practical things that glorify God and give Him joy on the journey.

A key principle I call "The Vicarious Life" is all about living your life *through* and *for* other people. The vicarious life can work for you or against you. It can result in selfishness or unselfishness. For example, suppose that when my son Luke was ready for college, I insisted that he go to Stanford. Why? Because I always wanted to get my degrees from Stanford. Luke could play sports there and fulfill dreams. But whose dreams would Luke fulfill? Mine.

Luke's desire was to attend Arizona State University. If Luke went to ASU and failed, my dreams would be crushed. Would it be Luke's fault? No. For I would have impacted my son with my dreams, not giving him a choice. I wanted a vicarious experience through my son. That is a selfish vicarious experience.

Suppose instead Luke was told I always wanted to have a degree, and if he chose to go to college, it would be wonderful, and the family would back him all the way. That would be a different story. That would be living the vicarious life unselfishly—for another.

Pastors and their boards are always asking me how to build great churches. I love helping them on my days off and following up on their progress. Through Pastors' School, I meet individuals whose lives are changed, and churches begin to grow for they catch the vision of winning souls.

I tell them stories of pastors who come from across the country, discouraged and weary in the work of the Lord. Then they get "caught" up in seeing what can be accomplished when we overdose on life—for the glory of God. When they leave Pastors' School, they take a piece of Phoenix First Assembly with them and leave a part of their grateful hearts on the mountain behind the church, where the last night they rededicate themselves to the work of God, to new dreams, goals, and visions.

Through their success and commitment stirred by the Holy Spirit, I reap part of their harvest. My happiness comes from watching them live out the dreams God gave me. I am asked the questions, Don't people disappoint you along the way? Aren't you risking a lot to pour yourself into people with the hope that they will go forth to win souls and heal hurts—and they don't? That is life on the fragile edge of a dream. The vicarious life puts you in a position of danger. When you invest yourself in another, the power is given to invalidate that investment. You can take what has been given you and squander the knowledge, teaching, and imparted vision. *You can kill the vision, but not the spirit of the visionary.*

This creates a challenge to reach out and find another to teach and encourage. Then be sure you are faithful to those who have invested in you. Paul expressed it like this:

> You therefore, my son, be strong in the grace that is in Christ Jesus. And the things which you have heard from me in the presence of many witnesses, these entrust to faithful men, who will be able to teach others also. (2 Tim. 2:1, 2 NAS)

One of my prayers had been to start a church in New York state. It doesn't look like I'm going to start a church in New York, a dream I once had for the inner city. But that doesn't mean that I haven't reached out to those in that tragic situation. Bill Wilson, a young man who was my bus director at the Westside Assembly of God in Davenport, Iowa, was called to New York.

This weekend Bill Wilson, will minister to about eight thousand little children in Brooklyn—kids he and his people will pick up in buses. He'll deliver children's sermons that he first developed while he was with us. God didn't send me to New York like I planned, but He allowed me to invest in the life of Bill Wilson. And through Yogi Bear Sunday Schools, Bill is impacting this generation for Jesus.

Annually we are required to send in our growth statistics to the denomination headquarters. Somehow our figures one year missed the deadline. Guess who led the fastest growing Sunday school in America! Bill Wilson—my former bus director! It is a *small* consolation that one year I won it, *vicariously!*

When you invest your life in other people, their accomplishments are yours. One of the boys who grew up under our ministry is pastoring in Miami. Two of our boys are spreading the gospel in Manila. Some are in South America. We have representatives in Mexico, Holland, and all over the world. I may never go to those places, may never minister to the people there or even see those churches—but because I invested in the lives of those people, I'm living their thrilling victories with them.

It seems like these days, wherever I go, I'm greeted by young people who have grown up in our church or sat under our teaching, and now they're in the ministry and doing great works for God. I'm hardly ever lonely when I get off a plane in a new city because one of those people will be there to greet me and bring me up to date on their ministry. And really, it's "our" ministry, because I'm able to live it vicariously through them. The amazing thing about all these extensions of our ministry—all these young preachers whose lives I've been privileged to invest in—is that I didn't give them a certain program to follow or a certain goal to live up to. We merely gave them the dream, a vision. It's part of the vicarious life. You don't have to fit the person into the mold you had for your life, you just have to share the dream.

Because our churches in Phoenix and Davenport have both claimed the title of fastest growing church in America at one time or another— and the Phoenix church has claimed it several times—people often ask me about our five-year plan or our-ten-year plan. Truthfully, we don't have one. We have what I call the one-day-at-a-time program rather than the five-year program or ten-year program. We believe that if we take care of the minutes, God will take care of the hours.

We do our best to care for the widows and orphans as God instructed us to. We worry about the present, and God takes care of the future. If you ignore the present, there will be no future. We don't live in the past—the past has no future.

I always encourage people when sharing dreams with others not to bind them to it down to the last detail. Let them grow into it—and you'll be surprised at the improvements they make in it! Your job in the vicarious life is to provide the opportunity and enjoy the experience as the other person lives it—not to orchestrate it.

Jesus lived the vicarious life, too, but in reverse—He looked to the future, at the torture of hell, and decided to dip His soul into it so that you and I would never have to. When we live the vicarious life, we make something good happen for someone else regardless of whether we had it ourselves. Jesus took something unthinkable upon Himself so that we would never have to. He suffered crucifixion and battled with Satan for the keys to death and hell so that you and I would not have to suffer a godless eternity. When we accept Jesus Christ and ask Him to forgive our sins and make us His children, we accept His vicarious experience. As Paul said, "We are crucified with Christ." Obviously, you and I were not *literally* crucified with Christ, but His experience is *vicariously* ours when we come to Him.

The miraculous thing about the vicarious life is this: When we experience a good thing vicariously, it's often even better than when we experience it ourselves—like my mental trips to the Grand Canyon. But when we experience something bad vicariously, it's never as painful and horrible as it is for the person who experienced it literally. We can say we are crucified with Christ, yet we will never know exactly how awful that experience was. Of importance is that Christ's experience on Calvary sufficed for all of us.

> He made Him who knew no sin to be sin on our behalf, that we might become the righteousness of God in Him. (2 Cor. 5:21 NAS)

> But as many as received Him, to them He gave the right to become children of God, even to those who believe in His name. (John 1:12 NAS)

3

A Sustainer of Vision

THE TELEPHONE RANG in my parents' home in Kansas City.

"Mother, I think I've fallen in love with a beautiful girl. I don't know whether I should ask her to marry me or not. I am in the ministry. She may not understand it all, for she is a new convert. It may be very difficult for her."

I was calling from California. I hesitated, then continued. "Will you let her come and stay with you and Dad for three months? That way she can see firsthand what the ministry is all about while I am overseas. You will know if she can take the pressures."

Anxiety burdened my heart—a heart that had been captured by a young model from Sweden. She had come to Christ in my evangelistic crusade during her first week in the United States. A former runner-up for Miss Sweden, Marja Kaarina Holmstrom and her friend had chosen to come to America so they could accomplish their dreams of becoming "stars." Their work visas were more realistic—admittance to the United States to be maids!

My totally supportive parents agreed to my request, and soon Marja was on her way, equipped with her postage-stamp-sized knowledge of

English and the emotionally turbulent baggage she carried within, invisibly labeled *the past.*

Marja was born in Helsinki, Finland, and her father was killed in the war. Her mother was left with a tiny daughter who was sickly from malnutrition and pneumonia. Marja's grandmother was an alcoholic, and to get money for her addiction, Marja's mother was forced to become a prostitute on the streets at fifty years of age.

Codependent before she walked, the waiflike toddler was eating from garbage cans, was passed from orphanage to orphanage, wandering in a maelstrom of the unknown. A product of frightening secrets and wartime scars, Marja—along with thousands of other victims—was subsequently shipped off to Sweden to be adopted. In Sweden, at six years of age, she was adopted by a wonderful couple. She received the best available smorgasbord of love and care. However, neither parent knew the Lord, although Marja was raised as a Lutheran. She describes her pastor as just another guy who loved to dance and make friends with people.

Her Swedish mother had told her to beware of mothers-in-law. They were her enemy. She was instructed not to trust them. With this background, Marja stepped off the plane to meet my parents and sister. She fit perfectly my description of the most beautiful blonde ever seen. Neither Mom nor Dad had trouble identifying what was to be their future daughter-in-law. My mom immediately loved Marja and treated her as a daughter. With everything new to Marja, and the life-style of a minister's family so different, the adjustment was not easy. Yet little by little, she understood that mothers-in-law were not "big, bad wolves," and she and my family grew close to one another.

Marja endeared herself to them with her Swedish/American language attempts that included clipped corners on words and scattered sentences. But most precious of all was her refreshing honesty and diligence to know God. Even our family doctor concurred after meeting her that I had chosen a "mother-image" for a wife. He proved to be a prophetic physician.

My mother Joy and Marja are like mother and daughter today. They truly love one another and often, unknown to the other, purchase the same items in a store. Joy has become her mother-in-*love.*

Marja's faith was greatly enhanced by her time in Kansas City, and the wedding plans were quick to follow. Though Plan A had been to marry an American millionaire or be a star, Plan B was the better plan of God. The former thoughts of a huge home and giant swimming pool dissolved into everything our marriage would be to her. She smiles today as she tells of her initial arrival in America, and the big limousine that picked her up at the Los Angeles airport and drove her to her Palo Alto, California, employment. The pretentious home portended good things to come, but the reality was soon visible. She was a maid, and the children she was charged with were precocious and undisciplined. It was only her stick-to-itive attitude that kept her there, and an innate sense that God had always had a plan for her life.

From a little girl whose treasure and focus of prayer was a small crucifix in her bedroom, Marja had felt the touch of the Almighty in the past, and would see His hand leading the future. "'For I know the plans I have for you,' declares the Lord, 'plans to prosper you and not to harm you, plans to give you hope and a future'" (Jer. 29:11 NIV). It was His hand that led her to a friendship with a Christian girl in Palo Alto. The friend asked if she would want to go to church to hear an evangelist. Reluctantly, she agreed. I was that evangelist. In church she could barely understand one word that was said. She was confused as to why the preacher got red in the face. Was he mad at the people? Her friend translated my fervor into her Scandinavian understanding. That same hand of God brought her back the second night of the series, and the Holy Spirit drew her to the altar to accept the Lord as Savior.

I ran down to meet her at the altar. (Now I'm sometimes teased about whether my zeal was carnal or spiritual.) Later I drove her home, and until 4:00 A.M. was praying for her and illustrating as best I could, with the language barrier, who Jesus was and that He could live in her life. Marja says it was the most beautiful night of her life. She was finally assured that the Lord Jesus was her Savior.

We had met in August and were married in December by my dad. Our honeymoon spanned Hawaii, the Philippines, Thailand, India, Sweden, and England. Storybook? Not exactly! It was foremost a missionary journey for me, and a unique and often troubling challenge to my beautiful bride. We lived in missionary homes, tents—with foreign food and more language barriers. It was a struggle, and Marja was being baptized with a fire she did not understand. A memory that resides with her was our hut in the jungles of India. This "honeymoon hotel" was a lean-to with a thatched roof shared with two indigenous houseboys. One boy was the cook, and the other skinned the animals we were to eat. The bathroom was a hole in the floor. In the evening, as we walked, we witnessed the dying and helplessly needy people covering the streets. Difficult? Yes! But also the birth of a compassionate heart that Marja has today for missionaries.

During those days each of my meetings included an altar call. Altar calls are a significant part of my ministry and have never been optional. Each time Marja would respond and come to the front to pray. Surrounded by nationals, this blonde woman was a dramatic contrast to those around her and the subject of much conversation. Marja explains that she knew she was a child of God, but had to keep affirming it in her heart.

The years wear well on this magnificent lady. She could easily represent Estée Lauder in commercials, but her truest beauty is centered from within. The grace with which she carries herself is an outward evidence of the grace of God that brought her salvation. Grace that begets graciousness and ultimate gratitude for all He is to her. "And after you have suffered for a little while, the God of all grace, Who called you to His eternal glory in Christ, will Himself perfect, confirm, strengthen and establish you" (1 Pet. 5:10 NAS). This was a promise of God she was unfamiliar with in those trying days in Finland.

Marja assumed the "mother role" with the birth of Kristie Kaarina. Following were Luke and Matthew. The family doctor had been right. She is a wonderful mother, and willingly devotes herself to caring for the children during my constant trips to serve the Lord. Marja has always sustained my visions.

She is quick to share that most people felt I would always be an evangelist, and was a bit surprised when I opted to join my father in Kansas City to be an assistant, a position I held for two years. Next came Davenport. She muses about her first glimpse of Westside Assembly: "It was the worst little building I'd ever seen." The congregation was the size of Phoenix First Assembly's bus drivers' fleet today—about seventy-six! But in five years, it grew to more than four thousand. She loved the people there, and was excited at watching my visions become realities.

With the church, her children grew. Marja has always been proud of our children. She says they are true pastor's kids that can sleep in the pew! Marja has been a willing advocate of the biblical implications of "Except the Lord builds the house, they labor in vain who build it" (Ps. 127:1). "Tommy is full of practical guidance," she warmly relates. "He is our pastor, too."

When institutions in our culture are constantly threatened, a pastor's family is under heavy siege and is not exempt from difficulties. We are aware our family is set in a glass house. Our "weather reports" include dilemmas, storms, and the flood stage of teenage issues, but the affirmations of love and godly dedications have allowed the whole family to remain strong with the church.

Kristie married young, and carries her drive and energy to her husband Kent Sexton's business. She is very aware she is rearing a sixth-generation champion for Christ. Luke, our oldest son, is at Arizona State University. He is good in sports and bright and faithful. His career considerations include business or church administration. He excels in kindness. Matt, the youngest, is a great fan of life. He would like to be a sportscaster or maybe do what I do. He also likes computers. At this stage it is uncertain what he will choose, but like all the Barnett clan, I pray they will bring God's love and more caring to this world.

With her perceptiveness, Marja relates she has seen God's ways of strengthening family ties even with my many absences. With the woman in Proverbs 31, she smiles at the future.

Marja's childlike faith started when she was in Finland and suffered from a painful stomach ailment. At that time, around four years old, she prayed God would heal it. He did. A series of other prayers strengthened her limited knowledge of the power of God, but *she used what she had experienced*. Prior to leaving Sweden for America, she knelt and asked God to have His way across the ocean. She confessed to not knowing what she wanted or needed and asked for help. God answered! In repeat performance.

When Luke, our first son, was four years old, he was playing in the garage and drank some antifreeze. He came into the house, coughing and sick. Marja recalls saying, "Lord, what am I going to do?" She had faith. Then she remembered Mark 16:18 NAS: "They will pick up serpents, and if they drink any deadly poison, it shall not hurt them; they will lay hands on the sick, and they will recover." She claimed that Scripture. Luke stopped coughing and returned to the yard to play. Everything was fine—until I got home!

Luke met me by boasting, "Daddy, I drank some gas." I became paranoid because Marja had not taken the child to the hospital. I called the doctor, who was angry—for she was sure Luke's kidneys and other organs would be impaired. Marja kept saying that Luke was all right.

Off to the hospital we went. Luke was there for almost a week and after every test he was diagnosed perfect. Nothing was wrong.

Today we smile if the weather grows cold. Luke doesn't freeze up!

Through a series of health problems, Marja has claimed the healing of the Lord and found Him adequate. She is assured that "the Father who hears in secret" does reward. Marja has faith for healings in a strong way. She will pray for the sick, spend a night in prayer to support a friend or member. Her faith is centered in believing God for those who need a touch from God.

Members of both congregations love and admire Marja. They appreciate the fact that she is a private person and independent—one who was made in heaven for her husband. Her sincerity is applauded. "Happy are the utterly *sincere*, for they will see God" (Matt. 5:8 PHILLIPS, emphasis added). "Blessed are the *pure in heart;* for they shall see God" (Matt. 5:8, emphasis added).

Sincere and *pure of heart* would be part of the portrait of Marja. Not that purity represents perfection, rather it is the genuineness and competency that surrounds her. She savors small moments when I am home, but accepts the times (most of the time) when I am at church or on a mission. She supports me with prayer and affirmation that being away is okay, which is a rarity in many pastor's wives' feelings.

Being visible and the focus of attention in such a large congregation could create problems. Not for Marja. She knows she was called to be "Tommy's wife." She fulfills her role with autonomy and opinion, but also recognizes the need for the biblical "covering" of her husband. With pride she remembers that in our other churches I would often drive forty-five minutes each way to spend just a few minutes with my family before having to return again. Although we have experienced many tough times together, her love has given her the strength to support me and let me accomplish that to which I have been called. Marja believes I am not just her husband, but her pastor, too.

She relates the years it hurt her when she returned to her birth mother and found her remarried. Her stepfather was an alcoholic, and very abusive. She watched one night when, while drunk, he tried to kill her mother with an axe. From this she developed a fear of men that lasted into her teens.

From me she learned that you must not look back, for *the past has no future.* Early she recognized life is made of choices, and you choose to be the kind of person you want to be. Attitudes are the same. We choose our attitudes—*to be bitter or be better.*

Today it is seldom heralded that pastoral marriages are special. Not perfect, but special. For us the love of God permeates our lives. And truly, we love each other.

Marja's friends and I could frame a portrait of her in this freestyle version of Matthew 6.

Happy is the woman who is honest with herself, with others, and above all, with her God. This woman has given over every conscious area of her life to God, and has asked Him to reveal to her the inner areas of fear and bitterness that need to be healed. Between her and her husband and friends there is no barrier. In her there is no tension, for she seeks to hide nothing from God or man. Because she is a transparent person, her Lord is able to shine through her life and be visible to those around her. (*Guideposts* magazine, © 1968 by Guideposts Association, Inc., Carmel, NY 10572)

Marja came to America, to become a star and she is! One that shines brightly and beautifully for the Lord. Several years ago she had the joy of leading her adoptive mother to the Lord. In May 1989 her atheistic father, just before his death, opened his heart to Christ, as she held his hand and led him in the sinner's prayer in a hospital in Sweden. Through Marja we are all reminded: "And they that be wise shall shine as the brightness of the firmament; and they that turn men to righteousness as the stars forever and ever" (Dan. 12:3).

4

Love Across
the Generations

"One generation shall praise Thy works to another, and shall declare Thy mighty acts. My mouth shall speak the praise of the Lord: and let all flesh bless His Holy name forever and ever." (Ps. 145:4, 21)

A GROUP of Christian psychologists were discussing specific families in their care. They had been diligent to do several generational studies on these people to search for clues and expressions of why the compounding, serious problems. Why the break-ups? Why the addictions?

One spoke up with a question that no one could answer, either personally or from their comprehensive files. *Why is Christianity not self-propagating* in so many church-related homes? God ordained the family to be "fruitful and multiply." His intent was not just as progenitors, but living illustrations of the reality: "For the Lord is good, His mercy is everlasting; and His truth *endures to all generations*" (Ps. 100:5, emphasis added).

Possibly the five generations in this chapter will give some insight as to what results when people *choose* to walk with God and instill simple, diligent, godly principles into the lives of their children. With a sixth generation now on the scene, my heart cries out for families to be whole and homes to be sanctuaries of the living Lord for generations until the Lord returns.

My study reveals a powerful thread throughout the generations. It could be called *love across the generations*—love for each other and love for Father-God.

SACRIFICE AND MORE THAN "REASONABLE" SERVICE

My paternal grandparents were good people and had an influence on my life. I remember them well and fondly. My grandmother, Ruth Barnett, was a Pentecostal from her earliest years. She had been Bible-taught and loved God. The man she married was a very strong Baptist. There were sharp contrasts between the two, but the union was rich and rewarding as they "sought God together." Ruth Barnett's decision for Christ came from a Pentecostal meeting in the oldest tradition, and her focus and faith were always a source of strength and devotion. Her influence was greater on their children than that of her husband, though he remained stalwart. Friends and relatives were proud that Mrs. Barnett was a first cousin to President Woodrow Wilson's second wife.

I never knew my mother's father—he died when she was eleven. Her paternal grandfather was an Englishman who came to America and became the pastor of a large, historic Presbyterian church. Her paternal grandmother, a lovely woman, came from Sweden. (History does repeat itself and comes into focus, for what occurred in the past impacted the present: I—a minister of the gospel four generations later—married another beautiful girl who came from Sweden. The gracious providence of God spans oceans!) Two years later, my grandmother Ollie Graves remarried and became Ollie Patten, and she was a wonderful influence on me. I remember her as a cultured, refined, and gentle lady. She loved the Word of God, and often the two of us would talk about its meaning and discuss the Book together . . . me, the wide-eyed listener, and my grandmother, the seasoned believer. It was evident she fulfilled her spiritual role, like the biblical Lois to me, her true grandchild in the faith. "For I am mindful of the sincere faith within you, which first dwelt in your grandmother Lois, and your mother Eunice, and I am sure that it is in you as well" (2 Tim. 1:5 NAS).

I also cherished this grandmother for she knew the way to a kid's heart was through his stomach—she relished the times I came to visit and always prepared things I enjoyed. She wore her pride on her sleeve and looked at me, her first grandson, as one who had unusual wisdom and caring for my years. She felt my youthful words of wisdom and insight often enriched loved ones and helped them along the way, in spite of the great span of years.

This grandmother loved art. She had appreciation for beauty and things with aesthetic value. She had an ear for music. I was greatly blessed as all of these traits found their way into me. My parents were from a generation of solid stock. "The lines are fallen unto me in pleasant places; yea, I have a goodly heritage" (Ps. 16:6). There is a heritage appointed by God, and this lineage was divinely programmed many generations ago!

My grandmother Ruth reflected Lois in the Bible. My mother Joy was abundantly blessed with the "Eunice profile," only set in a more contemporary surrounding.

A Mother's Perspective

When asked the question, "Did you ever intuitively know that your first child may be destined for God's service?" Joy responds thoughtfully, "I thought about this quite extensively, and I really cannot remember an incident when I knew Tommy was destined for God's service. It was a series of things that, at the time, passed almost unnoticed. I was very young when he was born. We lived in Electra, Texas, and I was at his aunt's home because we felt we could not afford a doctor in the hospital. The family stood in awe at the end of the room when he was born. When they saw the tiny infant they said, almost in chorus. 'We don't understand this, but we feel this is a special child, and his life-style will be a special life-style that somehow will be cut out by God.'

"At the time, this barely registered. I knew all mothers were overjoyed with their blessed events, and because we were Christians, we already knew that Tommy was special to God and would fit into His service somewhere. That was the desire of our heart and our mutual desire for our children.

"Later on when he was in kindergarten, one of his teachers became ill and underwent surgery. Tommy kept insisting that I go and visit her in the hospital. I finally responded to his childlike tug on my heart and visited this teacher.

"She said to me, 'Mrs. Barnett, I don't know what Scripture meant when it spoke of a child being a proper child. But I feel this way about your son Tommy. Not that he is perfect in school and in his ways, because he is a normal child. It is something in his nature, in his makeup, that I don't quite understand, a quality which is new to my experience. I believe God has His hand on that young life.'"

Mrs. Barnett, Sr., spoke on. "I was amazed that a secular schoolteacher would feel this way. And then as time began to unfold and various incidents came to my mind, I could see that God was very definitely working in his life in a profound way. I saw this little boy gradually begin to expand, to grow, and to mature in the direction of being definitely led of God, increasing 'in wisdom and stature, and in favor with God and man' (Luke 2:52), even as Jesus did as a child.

"Don't misunderstand me. He was never an idol of any kind. Much to the contrary. He was small for his years, and the normal teenage pressure to 'be good' and 'great in athletics' was a motivation for him, but not always a reality. Because of his size, he would try harder than most. My husband and I had placed in his heart an attitude of *'it can be done,'* and showed him as best we could, by example, that *nothing was impossible with God.*

"It is a family trait to mature a bit later in life, on our branch of the family tree. So, when he was in junior high school and high school, he was too small to play football, basketball, and some of those sports that enamored him. He was fascinated with track and field, and because he had fairly long legs, he determined he could run really fast and develop strong endurance. This he did and quite successfully. Even when it became a struggle because the others kids were taller and bigger than he, and he was forced to double up on his 'go power,' he achieved a remarkably fine record in school events. He also thrived on being manager of the basketball team. Even though he mainly carried towels!

"He could always depend on his dad to be there at any event to encourage him. We both were proud of every accomplishment. We even allowed our pride to show!

"I look back at some of the character-building times in his life that may appear insignificant, but were indicative of the character we sought to develop in each child.

"On one occasion, he had been given a little baby duck for Easter. As do all small children, he loved that duck and took very good care of it until it became a good-sized duck, possessing a mind of its own. When Tommy occasionally let the duck roam free in the backyard, his feathered friend would go over the fence into the neighbor's yard. We were frequently called to retrieve the duck and keep him permanently on our side of the fence.

"The neighbor lady was very angry with us because the duck kept getting into her yard. One day she said to me, 'If you don't keep that duck out of our yard, I am going to pull its head off and throw it in your yard.'

"The inevitable occurred. The duck flew over the fence for another adventure in neighborland, and the resentful lady kept her word.

"On our return from church, we found a dead duck. Tommy was so distraught, he resorted to verbal revenge—he told her, without using profanity, how disappointed he was in her, that he loved that little duck, and how her action broke his heart. (This might have been one of his first passionate sermons to an unwilling listener!)

"Later when his father came home that evening, the neighbor lady accosted him in the front yard and chewed him out—telling my husband what a bad father and terrible minister he was and what an atrocious son he had. She was horribly uncouth to him.

"My husband pondered it all in his heart and then told Tommy he would have to go next door and make a formal apology. After two failed attempts to make it next door, he obliged, but the apology was belligerently refused.

"However, he learned a lesson. The lesson of discipline and the lesson of obedience to his father. He also was perceptive enough to see the results, at a later date, of 'putting on kindness.' Subsequently, this same neighbor needed our family's help, and called to apologize for her attitude. My husband officiated at her husband's funeral, and I also sang for it. Tommy was there as a little child, showering her with kindness.

One is never too young or too old to have the Lord "Create in me a clean heart . . . and renew a right spirit within me" (Ps. 51:10). A Christian *never* has the right to have a wrong spirit. And a preacher's kid is never afforded that luxury!

"Most preachers have a rough day on Sunday. This is the one day he pours himself into all the services and gives God the best that is within. This is the day pastors and their families spread themselves razor thin. God's day was, for us, the busiest day of the week, carrying into late hours on Sunday night. Thus Monday morning could be trying as another week started."

One particular Sunday night Joy Barnett remembers "was a very, very late night. Tommy was put to bed in the wee hours. Monday dawned and we were up early, as usual. Getting Tommy ready for school that morning was a chore. He was listless and tired, and I kept urging him to eat his breakfast. His shoes were untied and I knew he would trip on them. I pushed and shoved as all moms do on occasion, to get him all together. He was slow to complete the routines of brushing his teeth and starting his breakfast. (He has never been a breakfast eater.) I tried to encourage him, but I was getting impatient.

"Every step was laborious. I had to encourage, and sometimes I was impatient. My nerves were on edge, and I was tired and irritable with him. I kept saying, 'Tommy, you are going to be late for school. You will never get there on time. You have only a few minutes. Now you are pushing it.'

"I finally got him out the door. I sat down, completely inundated with guilt. 'Oh, God. How can I be so impatient with my son?'

"Suddenly I heard his little steps coming back through the kitchen door. It was Tommy. He ran into the room, threw his arms around me and, in tears, he said, 'Oh, Mother, please forgive me for being such a bad kid this morning. I couldn't go to school until I came back and asked you to forgive me.'

"We both hugged and kisses were showered around. We were *so* sorry. We all loved each other and wanted clear channels of communication. Tommy raced out the door one more time, me praying all the way he would get there before the final bell, and he had a smile on his face.

"A song came to mind—maybe not the exactly right words, but the thought was paramount:

A song isn't a song until you sing it.
A bell isn't a bell 'til you ring it.
And love isn't love, any old day
Until you have it and give it away.

"My grandparents had given that love to my parents. Now I had a new burst of it to shower on Tommy, and most remarkably, he was the instigator, as a tiny boy that ill-fated morning, to continue the flow of love across the generations.

"Recently I asked him some of his childhood recollections. His first response was, 'Mother, I remember the long, cold Kansas City nights, and coming home from church at night in the bitter winter cold. Daddy would bring the car around on the snow and ice, and he often warmed the car for us before we got in. It took a long time to get the heater circulating warm air, but then you would slip into the car and put me on your lap and fold that old fur coat of yours around me, holding me close. I felt warm and loved and secure. And Mother, you always smelled so good.'

"It is easy in the daily-ness of living to forget the little things that mean so much to our children. The things of which memories are made. Things they will pass on to their family.

"Putting God first was a priority in our house. This was not always easy. When Tommy was born, he was very small. At about three months, he almost died with double pneumonia. We were staying with his grandmother on his father's side. My husband had to go on to revival meetings. Tommy was small and delicate, so I stayed behind to take care of him. He became very, very ill. He had bronchial pneumonia, which grew worse. The doctors told us he probably would not survive. We called his father who was in a citywide, sweeping revival in Illinois where many, many souls were being saved.

"We talked with him about coming home. He talked with God about coming home or staying there and closing the revival on the scheduled date. God gave my husband a definite impression that he should stay in the revival, that his little son would be all right.

"I was not happy with his answer at first. I felt that he belonged at home with us. However, he said he was praying definitely that God would touch our son, that he would get better. Our pastor in Electra, Texas, came to pray with us and 'peace like a river' settled on our home. All that night, as I held my little boy and prayed for his recovery, I *knew* he would get better. In the morning there appeared to be no change. In the afternoon the doctor came again. He assured us Tommy was on his way to recovery. Again we learned to live 'by faith, not by sight.'

"Tommy's father was a very strong preacher who never minced words. In a Sunday morning sermon, when Tommy was about four or five years old, he painted a picture of eternity—clearly designating that it is either with God in heaven or without God in hell. The little guy's heart was impressed. He wanted to know for sure that he was going to live in heaven someday, and that heaven was his certain destination.

"On the way to dinner after church, we drove across a bridge spanning a Kansas City river. Tommy, riding in the back seat, said, 'Oh, Daddy, I don't want to miss heaven. Am I a Christian? Am I saved?' And his father said, 'Tommy, you have always been a Christian. You gave your heart to the Lord from the beginning, as long back as we can remember.'

"Tommy was not satisfied with that answer, and his father added, 'Well, if you want to pray when we get home, we will talk about this and pray together.'

"Tommy persisted, 'But Dad, you said that people should not wait, that they should give their hearts to the Lord *now!*'

"I remember climbing over into the back seat with my son and right there, in that moving vehicle, he gave his heart to Jesus Christ as we were on the way to dinner. Now he knew for sure that his heart was right with God, and that his commitment was firm and established forever. He would join God in heaven someday.

"The years passed. At church one night when he was about nine years old, he sent someone to call me. He was kneeling at the altar. He looked up at me with those big blue eyes just shining and a beautiful 'shekinah glory' on his face. 'Mother, I have to tell you something. Someday, I'm gonna' make you so proud of me.' He kept emphasizing the statement. Not with pride, but with a commitment barely discernible, yet tightly sealed within.

"I was already proud of him, yet something within me registered that day that this child was telling me something a bit prophetic—his nine-year-old heart had been responsive to the Holy Spirit. I believe in that moment he felt 'the call of God' on his life. He may or may not have known exactly the field of endeavor in which he would serve, but he knew then, and in my heart, I understood.

"Somehow Tommy and I have always shared intuitive understanding and communication. His father was his hero—his role model. But it seemed to me that mine was to be the gentle influence. My role was to undergird them both. I don't want you to think ever that I was the meek, mild, little woman in the background. My husband would never allow that. He always pushed me to the front, and often required me to do things that I felt were beyond my ability. But because he believed in me, he knew I could do it, and I went out there and tried a lot of things that, perhaps on my own initiative, I would have never tackled. I did various things in the community and served in many capacities in the church. Tommy, through that, has learned to have great respect for women in the changing roles of their lives. He respects their strength of leadership as well as their gentle influence.

"His father was a strict disciplinarian. We gave Tommy music lessons. He hated to practice. I'm sure Tommy would tell you that his neglect of practice incurred more disciplinary action than perhaps any other area. I remember after Tommy was grown and pastoring his first church in Davenport, his father wrote to him and apologized for the strict enforcement of piano practice. Now, as he looks back on it, Tommy has often said 'I appreciate those times of discipline. I was a strong-willed little boy, and I can see that I needed it.'

"Tommy did learn to play the piano, the organ, the accordion, and the trombone. Sometime in his early years he would fill in on the organ or the piano in the absence of the church musicians.

"Never a braggart, Tommy was very reticent to tell us about anything outstanding that had happened to him. He sort of let us find out on our own. At one time when he was in junior high school, he played in the school orchestra. I was invited to come see a very special program. To my amazement, he was first-chair trombone in the orchestra. Until he stood up to play a solo I had not realized how well he could play. He had not told me. This is indicative of Tommy's nature. He went out there, did his very best, and rarely bragged about it.

"Tommy always had a prayer list. People would say, 'Pray for me,' or he would see a need somewhere and write each down on his prayer list. Every night before going to bed, he would kneel and call each name and each need aloud to God in his prayer—including the woman who killed his duck. This was when he was quite young—perhaps ten years old. Often his father or I would go into the bedroom and find him asleep on his knees, and we would lift him up and tuck him into bed. To him, knowing Jesus Christ, and his commitment to His will, was a very serious thing. Yet he was happy, active, with many friends.

"Tommy's cousin Jack Burgess recalls when he was ten and Tommy was eight years old, and they shot marbles between the cracks of Grandma's screened porch. When Tommy was losing, he would nonchalantly rub the marble on his head. Almost immediately his luck would turn and, much to his cousin's chagrin, the younger Barnett would win. (It was later discovered he was praying.) Every glass of water Tommy would bless, with thanksgiving to God!

"Early on he determined to give his energies to the things he could do best. He became president of his class, president of the student council, did well scholastically, and was an honor student."

Joy Barnett continues with obvious pride, minus any glory that would go anywhere but to the Lord. "We practiced the Bible model of Proverbs 22:6, 'Train up a child in the way he should go, And when he is old he will not depart from it.' "

Tommy's sister Vickie was born seven years after him. Vickie's recollections of Tommy are joyful. She says, "He was never a buddy, just a 'special, wonderful, talented, cool brother.' "

By the time Vickie was nine, Tommy was out in the ministry as a budding evangelist. Vickie recalls a trip the family took to visit one of his revival meetings in the Bahamas. Tommy was introducing each member of his family, and he said, "It is such a treat to have my sister here. Vickie, stand up and say a word."

Quickly, Vickie was on her feet saying, "It's a real privilege to be a treat." Her comment brought the house down. She remembers the event because of the extreme embarrassment the occasion caused her. Today Vickie is an accomplished person in her own right. She is a soloist, speaker, musician, choral director, produces pageants and cantatas, and works with the youth in her church. She has earned a master's degree in education, is an outstanding high school teacher, and has won many awards and trophies for her contributions to the community. Living with her husband and five children—three her own, she continues the "self-propagating" element of real Christianity.

Joy Barnett loved the visits of her grandchildren. Especially Kristie and Luke in the days before Matthew was born. One of her fond memories of "this fifth generation" was one day when she was sitting in the family room. Her windows were open onto the patio where Kristie and Luke were playing. She was observing their play.

They had found a tired bouquet of wilted roses that had been given to her the Sunday before. The children had taken these roses and on the floor of the patio had made the shape of a Christmas tree. They had discovered little trinkets and wrapped them and put people's names on them. Then pleased with their work, they announced, "This is Christmas at Grandmother's!" To them, this tree was a work of beauty. To Grandmother, a tribute to all the work that made Christmas special in the past—now forever etched in her heart. This simple gift from her grandchildren brought heartfelt meaning.

Why the emphasis on some of the "little things" of life? The Bible reminds us to "despise not the day of little things." *Faithfulness* and *example* are pillars in establishing families. Example is not just one thing. It is everything. Bringing up children in the Lord is more than occasional trips to church and Sunday school.

In Genesis 12 the Bible tells us that Abraham built an altar to God. In Genesis 26 his son Isaac does the same thing. It would have been easy for Abraham and Sarah to have *told* Isaac the benefits of worship, of working for God, and of trusting God, or even to have sent him off to a Tent City boarding school to receive instruction. Instead he was trained by watching and emulating his father and mother.

A Sunday school survey notes that 60 percent of boys drop out of Sunday school with the excuse, "My dad doesn't attend, so, can it be that important?

To Abraham it was. And to the Barnetts, faithfulness and example were never optional traits.

When we give, even beyond our limits, we receive so freely in unique and surprising ways.

TRUSTING GOD ANEW PUT TO A TEST

Kristie and her cousin Danielle were staying all night with their grandparents on June 16, 1983, the night that Hershel Barnett, my father, totally unexpectedly graduated to his eternal reward. That night and morning would change the lives of all us Barnetts.

Dad's death brought a "gap" in the hedge of Christianity. He had fallen like a tower, and the landscape of the lives of those who loved him would never be the same.

Although God's children are not to question His providence, it is hard to fathom His timing. People are immortal until it is God's time to take them. Charles Spurgeon wrote during his last illnesses, "Grieve not when I die. For this was I born."

Hershel Barnett was one of the spiritual giants of his generation. He was a man who captured the hearts of his people, and kept Kansas City "clean" for scores of years by continually opposing alcohol. His controversy with the city on "liquor by the drink" made the papers. He and his church tried to keep the liquor issue off their county's ballot. It was unsuccessful. However, since that particular election, the Kansas Supreme Court nullified the vote.

"The politicians deal with liquor as a glamorous issue," my father would way. "They tend to see it as a way of getting reelected. We see it as a moral issue. I have dealt with alcoholics on skid row. I have seen it take milk off the tables and result in broken homes."

Although my dad fought for many spiritual rights, his major issue was always humanity's relationship with God. Politicians and publicans were his friends. Rich and the poor people flocked to his parish. The newspapers heralded him as a totally "people-oriented man."

For forty-three years he had pastored Victoria Tabernacle. Neither flood nor fire dampened his drive for God. In 1951 a major flood devastated his church, and years later a fire leveled it to the ground. He was often in the center of controversy—never on the fringes of disbelief.

People in Kansas described him as "the man who always came back." They were amazed at his durability and stability and growing spheres of influence in both the secular and Christian world. He was an encourager, an unpredictable pastor, a visionary, and had a way of causing hearts to smile. He was a competitor and leader of men. He challenged scores of young men into the ministry—one being me, his only son.

He collected friends like people collect treasures. He knew them well and was concerned for their needs. He would walk into a restaurant and talk with everyone there—whether they had been introduced or not. Everyone was a friend or a friend waiting to be met.

My dad had a way of becoming involved with everyone. He made people feel they were important and special. His strong convictions were respected, although not always agreed with in the marketplace.

Unlike the usual portrait of a pastor, he served four terms as a member of the Kansas City Board of Education. He ran two times as a candidate for mayor. He was an avid sports fan, and he held one of the longest records of handball playing in the city. Beginning in 1946, on Mondays and Fridays, he was on the handball court, always playing with a longtime friend. Friends observed he played handball well, but when it came to the devil, he played "*hard*ball." He pitched for three church baseball teams. He played right up to the time of his death at sixty-eight years old. Dad often remarked that "I come from a very righteous line of people. I was called at a very young age to serve God. My mother's father was a Church of Christ preacher. On my father's side, my great-grandfather started the First Baptist Church in Decatur, Texas."

This was another indication of a godly legacy that had been established. Surely he was aware of God's promise regarding His future generations: "I will pour out My Spirit on your offspring, And my blessing on your descendants" (Isa. 44:3 NAS).

TO LIVE IN HEARTS WE LEAVE BEHIND IS NOT TO DIE

There was an irreplaceable emptiness in my heart as I flew to Kansas City with my family to preach my father's funeral service. The tie that bound my dad and me together had the tensile strength of steel. My father shared so much of his life in the years of our bonding together.

I had been an eyewitness to the work of God through my dad, and a symbol *to* my dad of God's faithfulness generation to generation. "The living, the living, he shall praise thee, as I do this day: the father to the children shall make known Thy truth" (Isa. 38:19).

When I was in my parents' home, prior to the memorial, I went to my dad's closet. There I discovered two suits hanging on the rack. One was an old threadbare gray suit, the other a contrast in shiny black. The black suit was not mohair, but shiny from having been pressed a thousand times over the years. In the closet were shoes. Shoes with cardboard in the soles. You would have to deduce that the soles had trodden a heavy and long path for souls. After all, God never described the condition of His children's shoes when he proclaimed, "How beautiful upon the mountains are the feet of him that bringeth good tidings, that publisheth peace; that bringeth good tidings of good, that publisheth salvation; that sayeth to Zion, *Thy God reigneth!*" (Isa. 52:7, emphasis added).

I knew my dad did not have to live that way. He had pastored one of the biggest churches in the city. My mother was active for the Lord and always looked like a model. But things and clothes and material trappings were insignificant to Hershel. Other things took precedence.

In the early dawn of the day of the funeral, I drove to the church to meditate and pray. It was about 4:00 A.M. As I quietly walked into Victoria Tabernacle and moved toward the front, I became aware of other people. The casket was lying in state in front of the pulpit. It was dark except for an eternal candle that flickered in the front. As the candle lit my path toward the steps that led to the platform, I caught a glimpse of a young man kneeling in prayer. Turning, I noticed people had already preceded me into the sanctuary. They were young men, young preachers and students, crying and praying—spending one more night with the old prophet.

The deacons had taken turns throughout that night to sit with him as a symbol of respect and love for not just their pastor but their friend. When the services began, the church overflowed. The grief was obvious, yet the "Healer of broken hearts" was ever-present. Tears flowed like a river, but the rainbow of God's love and faithfulness reached from Kansas City to Glory. Like an ark, symbolizing the covenant of God from here to eternity, it was a reminder that "this God is our God forever and ever." And Pastor Hershel Barnett was forever with his Lord.

If the eyes have no tears, how can they behold God's rainbow of promise that declares: "I am the resurrection, and the life: he that believeth in Me, though he were dead, yet shall he live: And whosoever liveth and believeth in Me shall never die" (John 11:25, 26).

Profiling the crowd was easy. There were youngsters *en masse* to say goodbye to their friend. Hershel's grandson Drew, eleven, and very special to his granddad, took a piece of candy to place in Granddad's pocket as he was lying in state. The undertaker tenderly lifted Drew up to deposit the candy—symbolic of the treats that had been passed out to multitudes of kids. Hershel Barnett was a champion of little people of all sizes, shapes, and colors.

A blind man came with his dog. He had been a park person and had an abiding friendship with his pastor. His seeing-eye dog had always loved Reverend Barnett. His owner asked if he could take the dog up for one more look at "his best friend. You see, my dog loved the preacher." Again, the wise deacons concurred.

People flocked for one more opportunity to show love and respect for Hershel Barnett. Men in baseball uniforms held their caps over their hearts—for my dad had pitched a doubleheader three days before his death. A few days later they retired number sixty-five, his uniform number. However, the team all knew they could never retire the good that he had done for them, his church, and Kansas City.

The thought of my dad pitching brought warm memories into my mind. It appeared that the league had instituted a rule when the senior Barnett was sixty-five years old and having difficulty running the bases. The new rule was, upon reaching sixty-five, it was permissible to bat, then substitute another player to run the bases. I always wondered if that rule had been made up just for my dad. If that had been the case, my dad would have never allowed it—but that was the degree of love the team had for their pastor-pitcher.

At the funeral, a mentally handicapped woman came up to grieve and to ask a question, "What will I do now that your dad is gone?" She related that he himself had always come by to pick her up for church on Sundays. Here was the pastor of a huge church with a fleet of buses, going every week to bring a carload of people to church himself, and then take them home in the afternoon. "I wouldn't ask anybody to do anything I'm not willing to do myself," he would say.

The mayor of Kansas City was at the service. Senator Bob Dole was there, surrounded by the city council and the school board. The guests formed a line so long to greet the family that they stood for more than eight hours to shake hands and receive condolence. Still many never made the front of the line.

As the procession moved from the church to the cemetery, the way was lined with merchants standing at attention in front of their businesses. For blocks people stood in honor as Dad passed by. Friends or foe, they all had respect for my father. Some shops closed. Others had signs saying "Good-bye" or "Rest in Peace." It was a day to remember.

The crowd and diversity of population did not surprise me at all, because my dad knew everybody in town. He used to go down to the truck stop and drink coffee with the truckers in the morning. He was the kind of person who would walk into new surroundings and greet everyone in sight. All around the city and state, he was known as "Barnett the Preacher," the man who kept Kansas a dry state for so many years. He pastored his church for forty-three years—a record in our denomination.

Dad always told me he would never retire—doing God's work was his primary motivation. He never changed. Right up to the final Wednesday night when he preached a sermon, went home and set his alarm for 5:00 A.M. so he could play handball. He never woke up. "Absent from the body, present with the Lord."

They were never quite sure why my father died—heart failure, maybe, they told me. However, I am convinced he just died from an *overdose of living*.

I became a preacher of the gospel because my father was a preacher. He was my mentor and my friend. I loved and respected him, and I wanted to do like he did. Growing up in a Christian home made me believe in God because my parents believed.

Each step of my life, I reported to my father, asked his advice, and received his praise. His accolades and approval were my reward. He poured out his wisdom to me in steady doses. His image was a touchstone always present, secured like a safety net around my life. He taught me the illustrated sermons that have become a staple of our ministry. He taught me about the living Christmas tree and the living cross. My mother pioneered many of the events we use today at Phoenix First Assembly, events that were born deep in Dad's well of resources.

Dad was my champion. My model. I watched him give everything he had to the church. I wanted to be like him.

Never doubt that I believed the things that I preached. I knew and had appropriated the gospel truths. Yet in many ways my ministry as an evangelist and in my churches is based on my father's vision and my father's revelation of God. We both accepted the New Testament pattern of a church, but even that pattern filtered through my dad.

We were so close. When my boys would make good plays in their sports, I'd come home and call my dad and proclaim the news that Matt had hit a home run or Luke had scored a touchdown. We burst with enthusiasm and pride in the hearts and minds of one another. When I had a decision to make, I would call him up and we would talk it over.

If my church experienced a big day, he would be waiting by the phone because he knew he would get a play-by-play account when it was over.

His death called up an unsettled occurrence within me. I was realizing from a new perspective that my spiritual life was also based on his. How would I go on without him? Who would be my counselor? I had spent years counseling other lives in turmoil, but now my personal, beloved counselor was gone. I pondered on who would be my fan club now? Besides my family? Who would I call on those big days? Who could I brag to? And more discouragingly, who would I phone on life's slow and difficult days when I needed the kind of encouragement that only my dad could give me?

Amidst the grief and struggle with personal loss, I came face to face with the foundation I had built my life upon. It was solid, but it was my father's foundation. Now that foundation had slipped away—forever. In that anxious moment of realization, there was an awesome revelation that was to be unveiled. For when I cried out, "God, who will I turn to now?" there was an answer: "When my heart is overwhelmed, lead me to the rock that is higher than I." (Even higher than the precious pedestal that held my dad.) God heard and God answered! It was crystal clear in my innermost soul, "You can turn to Me, Tommy. 'I have loved you with an everlasting love, with lovingkindness have I drawn you.' I love you even more than your father did. Now that he is gone, you will have to look beyond his revelation. You must search for your own."

In Isaiah 6:1, Isaiah wrote, "In the year that King Uzziah died, I saw also the Lord." Uzziah had been the prophet's friend as well as his king, but when Isaiah lost his friend, God stepped in Himself to console him.

The day my dad died, I began to see the Lord more clearly. With my champion fallen, I could no longer rely on another's strength and vision and wisdom. God stepped in to provide His strength and vision and wisdom. God provided a firsthand revelation of who He was and what He would be. No longer would I need to rely on my father. Like a blazing searchlight of truth, everything that had been preached for the majority of my life "turned on" like ten thousand watts of power. He understood it all. Because that is what happens when you have a firsthand experience with God.

I still believed as my father believed. I still preached as my father had preached, but now the only intermediary was the Father through His

Son and Holy Spirit. The awesome accomplishments for God today come because I not only have intellectual knowledge and paternal knowledge, but firsthand revelation—knowledge of the plan of salvation, prayer, and traveling the journey to the Promised Land—straight from God to me.

I will never forget my father. I want people to recognize his greatness and accomplishments. He was and will be the most unforgettable character I have ever met. I will always cherish his insight and vision. I may never stop looking heavenward, wishing for his prayers and encouragement.

After his death a major *re-vision* occurred. I learned to put aside the "former things" and allow God to let me behold His "new thing." Before I copied the copy. Now I knew *the* Original, and every day became a masterpiece fresh from eternity's storehouse!

PART TWO

*R*e-Vision

5

Selah Time

SELAH!—PAUSE AND THINK

SELAH INTRODUCES a pending "re-vision" of thought seventy-seven times in Scripture. Seventy-four times it appears in the Psalms and three times in Habakkuk. Selah represents a rest, like in music, a change, even a new sense of direction. Selah leads to active ministry, which cannot be envisioned without Selah time.

As I began to depend on God alone as my source, my resource, and my goal, the necessity of Selah time changed my life. Selah carries with it an ocean of meaning, but basically to me it says, "pause and think." To others it carries the thought of stopping to focus on God. To thank Him for His fellowship and communication. Thank Him that we can confess our sins, or praise Him; thank Him for all forms of communication with God, even to waiting on God. However, I am convinced the little five-letter word Selah is not talking to God. It is not even prayer. It is not confession. It is not thanksgiving. It is not even waiting upon the Lord.

I believe the pause-and-think meaning is saying we must learn to be quiet before the Lord.

In music a pause or a rest emphasizes the composer's heart for the music. "It offers variation and intensity. It gives respite to a certain character or mood of music established by its rhythm, dynamic level or harmonic structure. It provides opportunity for new and exciting entrances to subsequent passages." The Greeks called it "a little stop, the little pause in the song." This marking is vital to every score of music. As vital as the notes and chords.

So with believers Selah is used to illustrate the time when Christians take time to think. The holy writer said, "Be still, and know that I am God" (Ps. 46:10).

People who do not feel deep emotions are people who do not practice Selah time—"pause-and-think" time. I never lay my head on my pillow at night without recollecting the day's events. I visualize my family and the joy they are to me. I think of foreign countries where I have been and where people sleep on the open street. Sometimes I picture sights from Calcutta and Bombay and other cities in India, remembering a mother with a newly born child, a man dying with no one in attendance. Kids looking for any kind of garbage. Life on the impoverished streets of need.

I scarcely sit down to eat a meal alone that I do not think of the starving people I have seen, remembering ones who took meager handsful of grass seed to make a bit of porridge to fill their distended stomachs, while others with nothing looked hopelessly on.

Sunday morning preparation begins at 4:00 A.M. For an hour I seek God for the day that is ahead of me. Then I get into my car and drive to the city. I pass the homes of the poor and the rich, the schools and businesses, parks and playgrounds. I am getting ready to minister to my people.

When I come onto the platform I have been preparing for hours to preach. Part of that preparation is falling in love again with my people. It isn't hard when you have been practicing Selah time.

During the week I counsel people. I listen to their questions and problems. I hear their heartaches and share their joys. I sometimes watch them rush across the parking lot on Wednesday night, still fussing with the kids to be sure they look right for church. Some of these people work hard. Getting to God's house is a willing sacrifice.

Some Sundays I pause to watch the bus ministry people come into the bus lot to prepare the buses for the day. These are people with full-time, demanding jobs. Sunday could be their day of rest. Instead it is their busiest day. The burden of Sunday is heavy. But the burden is also light.

How can a burden be heavy and light? Only if you are yoked to God. In coming to Him on Sunday or any day, "the yoke is easy and the burden is light" if He is in command.

I am always honored by the presence of people who come to our church. Through Selah we lock hearts. We become "one in the Spirit and one in the Lord."

When God chooses to use a word seventy-seven times, it ought to attract our attention. If it is true that every jot and tittle is inspired and has a purpose, then certainly every word is likewise God-breathed.

The Lord's Supper is Selah. Not only do we come together to pray and confess our sins, this is God's effort to draw our attention to Himself so that we might *think* about Him. He stated that when we partake we do this "in remembrance of Me."

The psalmist asked the question: "What is man that thou art mindful of him?" It is the greatest wonder of the universe to know that God is mindful of us. Selah is any activity where we pause and become mindful of God and think about God and reflect on life.

The Bible says, "Study to be quiet" (1 Thess. 4:11). Another translation reads, "Concentrate on being quiet." God is saying we have to learn to be quiet. Discipline produces Selah.

Isaiah relates, "In quietness and confidence shall be your strength" (Isa. 30:15).

I meet people constantly who have no confidence. Some say life is too much of a struggle. Others have no strength to face their fast-lane pace. They shout, "Stop the world, I want to get off," but don't know how. Some are so nervous or addicted that they surrender to the inevitable— no hope. For all these circumstances I want to recommend Selah time. I do not believe people will be weak for long if they practice Selah.

Many of us need to know ourselves but we are afraid to be alone. The radio blares or the television accompanies us to sleep. Kids raise the decibels of the stereos and disc players. Few are taking the time to hear the voice of God.

Our modern, urban society is so busy rushing that we have lost what our founding fathers had. If you do not believe it, I want you to read a modern-day book and then read a book that was written fifty to a hundred years ago. The vocabulary and living descriptions of days gone by make our contemporary written word pale and sick. We are obsessed with designing cars, we've increased the high rises and towering buildings, and improved our electronics and science. However, when it comes to language, vocabulary, and literature, we have decreased tragically and the reason is we don't take time to *think* and create like we did in the past.

The old-timers had time on their hands to think as they walked and plowed the furrows of the field behind the donkey. We live in an age of fast-food, fast cars, the fast fix, and fast solutions to any problem. We don't even recognize the need to Selah.

God graciously gives us an awareness of the benefits of Selah. "Study to be quiet." I believe we would be shocked to know what our minds could come up with if we took time to write again. To just stop and think.

There is little difference between some of this book's readers and a Shakespeare, Tennyson, or Browning. The difference is measured in thinking time. The potential for greatness lies dormant in most people. I hear pastors say, "*There* is a deep thinker." It may be possible that that person is merely *a* thinker who takes time to muse.

It is tragic that researchers say the average person in a family rarely spends more than thirty minutes alone during the day. I am not talking about being alone with God, but being alone with yourself, then being alone with God and reflecting on Him and His goodness. "The effect of righteousness is quietness and assurance forever" (Isa. 32:17). Righteous people are affected by their righteousness. They want to be quiet and alone, away from the crowd for a time to become like Jesus.

In Psalm 42 David talked to *himself* in verses 1, 6, and 7. This sad but beautiful statement was written when he stopped for some Selah time. As he paused to think and remember the good times, when he led the processions into the temple, and the past experience of God's proven faithfulness, he could again call on God—his Rock—even though he was in trying times. From his Selah, David emerges as a man with a right relationship to his trial. For the grace of verse 8 triumphs over the trial of verse 7.

It may be a disquieting suggestion, but *poverty* is possibly one of the greatest blessings our children can experience for a time. I have seen poor kids who have nothing to play with and nowhere to go, create a lot of "somethings" out of their "nothings." They have been forced to be alone with their thoughts. They entertain themselves and become innovative. I fear our affluent children spin on the wheel of pleasures and leave little time to really think. God has been convicting me that we need to teach our young people to be quiet. Teach them to ponder and meditate. Show them the value of thinking deeply. Encourage them to put their thoughts on paper and then discuss them.

By necessity one of my children recently was forced in school, as a disciplinary action, to write an essay. I was given the paper to read, and I could not believe that it came from a Barnett. It was profound and great. I thought then how amazing and awesome people can be when they stop to think—when they Selah.

We need to teach our children to read. Tremendous Jones came up one day with an idea that he would give his boy a stack of books, and for every book that he read, he would give him five dollars. He said his son literally turned around. His mind learned to read and retain. Our lives are constantly challenged by what we read.

Mr. Jones relates, "You are the same today as you'll be in five years except for two things: the people you meet and the books you read!" Life-changing books are powerful encounters of the valuable kind. Diligent search to discover written sources of knowledge in broad fields increases vision and stretches our capacity to perform.

Encourage your children to be readers. Show them by example the benefits and discuss the books together.

How much more secure we would be if we took time for Selah. That is the place where there is more time to think about God. I never find *thinking* people who are insecure people. I have watched tense people relax and unwind as they take thirty minutes a day to meditate, then think about God and his goodness. Their whole demeanor settles down.

Walks are a wonderful way to think—taking in the beauty of the surroundings and quietly thinking. "And my people shall dwell in a peaceable habitation, and in sure dwellings, and in quiet resting places" (Isa. 32:18). How much more secure we would feel if we experienced more Selah time, knowing as we come from those times, our spirits will be blanketed with peace and quiet assurance.

In those moments we can reflect on God and be assured of His presence and care and love. Insecure people are not into Selah time. They prefer wallowing in their insecurities and phobias. Nervous people have difficulty sitting still for a time. Whatever the malady, thirty minutes of thinking, then considering God and His goodness, is the best nerve medicine around, coupled with walks that help us think as we go.

The reason we are short on theologians is our thinkers appear to be diminishing. Selah time would make a great impact in the Christian world.

Prayer is designed to be a scheduled, daily event and one of continuous flow. It is interesting, however, that God said His people must schedule a time to be quiet, so as to *know* Him. Both passages in the Bible that focus on success are accompanied with the essential ingredient of meditation.

> "Blessed is the man that walketh not in the counsel of the ungodly,
> Nor standeth in the way of sinners,
> Nor sitteth in the seat of the scornful.
> But his delight is in the law of the Lord;
> And in His law doth he *meditate* day and night"
> (Ps. 1:1, 2, emphasis added).

The motivation movers and the quiet success stories all hold a common denominator—a time of quiet. Meditation. Selah!

The Bible is saying if you are going to prosper and want to be successful you will have to learn to meditate. You have to practice Selah. Underscoring that criterion are the words of Joshua 1:8.

> This book of the law shall not depart out of thy mouth; but thou shalt meditate therein day and night, that thou mayest observe to do according to all that is written therein: for then thou shalt make thy way prosperous, and then thou shalt have good success.

Many people have labored in vain for accomplishments and have been run ragged by playing tag with success formulas. I believe God's plan is for His people to incorporate Selah. After all, God is the boss. We are all in His employment. No life is complete until this lesson is taken to heart, and that innermost heart knows God. Because that is when you discover that God truly *is*.

I have learned a lot of lessons by just looking at a tree—the beauty, the foliage, and spring budding. There is so much grandeur and uniqueness in a tree. No one will upstage Joyce Kilmer's classic poem "Trees." He was right—only *God* can make a tree. The psalmist wrote that the blessed and successful man "shall be like a tree planted by the rivers of water, that bringeth forth his fruit in his season; his leaf also shall not wither; and whatsoever he doeth shall prosper" (Ps. 1:3).

I believe that I am a pastor of trees. I look at my congregation as trees. I minister to my people as ministers. I am cultivating, watering, and speaking to trees. If I do my job, those trees will bear fruit. They will not wither and dry up when weary. When they are weary they will go out and win another soul, heal another hurt, and bear fruit. That kind of fruit remains and begets more fruit.

There is no drought for those trees, for they are watered by the Lord, through the Shepherd of the Forest.

> I thank my God that I can see
> Fruit evidence from Godly trees,
> Trees who lift their branches fair,
> And bring forth seeds of faith and care.
> Trees that let their roots go deep
> Through meditation, pure and sweet.
> Trees that drink from brooks above.
> And spread the fruit on wings of love.
> The foolish sometimes look to rhyme.
> The wise invest—in Selah time.

The pastor makes sure his trees or congregation are in good shape, that they are spiritually healthy with fruit. He is willing, if need be, to prune and cut back in order to produce great growth and additional premium fruit.

The man of God cultivates those trees with God's Word and the consistent message that Jesus Christ *is* God—the touchstone of our faith. That Jesus is more than enough. That the Holy Spirit is a person.

He tells the trees that Jesus is a healer. He cares for the lame, the halt, the blind, the needy. He shares the miracles that Jesus performed but reminds the "trees" that miracles are not the reason He came to earth. He came to glorify His heavenly Father and to forgive sins. Miracles are a by-product of His coming.

The trees are attended by the one that appropriates time to be alone with the True Vine and His heavenly Father, the Vinedresser. A hymn of antiquity crosses my mind.

> I come to the garden alone,
> while the dew is still on the roses;
> And the voice I hear, falling on my ear,
> The Son of God discloses.
> And He walks with me, and He talks with me,
> And He tells me I am His own.
> And the joy we share as we *tarry* there,
> None other has ever known.
> —C. Austin Miles

As I, at times, "tarry" with the Lord, I look at the trees and the magnificent Shadow Mountains surrounding our church and think, how beautiful. Only Creator God can make this scene.

There are times we brag on a wonderful artist's picture—for example, a beautiful oil painting of tropical palm trees. How gifted the artist must have been. How talented and creative. The rendering is so lifelike, almost as if we could feel a breeze rush through the branches. Outside the window is the real thing. A palm, in monochromatic green, stately, lofty, almost regal in beauty. We laud the artist while we have the Creator all around us.

Selah time focuses on the Creator.

People love to jog—the great American pastime is beneficial beyond bodily health. Mental health is improved. It is a time to think while moving and then rest when exhausted.

I hear people, "Boy, he is a brain," or "She is so creative." I believe the difference between mediocrity and greatness is not that the person has so many brains or is ultracreative, but rather the person has included Selah time in his or her life. God creates through people. Since He dwells in our spirit, we need to spend time feeding that spirit side of the inner man. Let the spirit soar!

One of my staff, Larry Kerychuk, has memorized a lot of Scripture. I hear our people talk about how gifted Larry is because of his memorization. Larry is gifted because he has learned the importance of Selah time. In those moments of meditation he listens and learns and is taught of God.

There are few difficulties or problems that Selah time would not improve or solve. Bitterness arises because people do not stop, pause, reflect, and get the whole picture. If we take time to walk in the moccasins of that individual, as the Indians said, and sit in their seats and think about it all—the bitter gets better and the crisis has a way of dissolving.

I have counseled hundreds of people who get bitter with God. If I could get them to take Selah time and reflect on what God has done for them, and all of the blessings He has showered on them—known and unknown blessings—the bitterness would disappear.

Selah time brings up another story. A sad story of when God looked down from heaven and saw people, lost, complaining, and without hope. How could a Holy God possibly reconcile to sinful man? How? He sent His Son to die on a tree. When that tree was cast over our lives, the bitter cup of sin and death passed by too, and sweetened each bitter "well" of life. (The Marah story is in Exodus 15.)

Marahs are included on life's journeys. Selah time puts them into divine perspective. Recently Marja and I went back to dedicate a church in Rockford, Illinois, about one hundred miles from Davenport. One morning we quietly drove by our former home. A surge of memories flooded us both with emotion. We walked to the three acres behind our old place and looked at a ball field the kids and I had used. I remembered a time during a game when one of my boys struck out and the other kept walking the players he pitched to. After that game the three of us worked on hitting and pitching until it was dark. I Selah'd. Marja and I walked to the creek where we used to fish for minnows. And we saw the pitch-and-putt golf course we made—the one that helped improve Luke's game so much that Dad never wins anymore. We both just allowed our minds to go back . . . back . . . back and remember when!

Often driving home I will go by a park close to our Phoenix home and look at the old basketball goal, where lots of hours were spent shooting baskets. The goal is a waving memory flag each time I drive by—and surrounding it, thoughts I hold close. There are memories of slam dunks, lessons in life, a neighbor kid's version of a full-court press, and our sometimes private free throw line.

People dash off to movies and try to find one that makes them laugh or cry. I prefer sitting in front of that basketball net and musing and meditating about the big things of life magnified on the silent screen of my mind. And life takes on more meaning.

People frequently ask me if I keep scrapbooks—if I have records of all the things that have transpired in my first half century of life. I tell them all the same thing. I am too busy making scraps to make a scrapbook. I keep things in a special memory book of my mind. I am afforded the luxury of opening that book and turning those pages at will—anytime, anyplace, anywhere!

Young people from our Pastors' School write letters telling me they are preaching my messages, telling my stories, and even getting a hoarse voice like mine. I tell them they are welcome to use all material, lots of which I got from great thinkers of yesterday. But I remind them all that if they don't watch out, they are going to miss the real secret, which is Selah. *Be still. Pause and think!*

Selah is used in another way in the Bible. It is used for emphasis. In Psalm 24, a great moment of crescendo rose as the people were reminded, "Who is this King of glory? The Lord of hosts, He is the King of glory. *Selah.*"

Often we reach great moments in our lives and fail to pause and Selah. After each service, I either return to my office for some Selah time or take some time at home. I shut the door on the world and recall everything that transpired and meditate for a time. I think about the music, the people, the anointing, the altar call. There is something about that pause that makes the passing event real. That pause fills my life with emphasis.

What a special event when a child graduates. When my daughter Kristie graduated, we had a party. We celebrated! After it was over, I went to my room and thought about my only daughter, who is now a wife and mother. I put her life on rewind and played back scenes that make parents glad. The first time she was an angel in a Christmas pageant, her first day of school as she skipped off with my heart in her pocket. I thought about her eighth grade graduation and when, for the first time, she made the honor roll. On her sixteenth birthday I rented a limousine and took her to an elegant restaurant. It was a wonderful surprise. Life holds an abundance of magic moments. We have only to look for them.

A Selah that is not as familiar to our thinking is the Selah used in the songs for response to great depths of despair and moments when we walk through the valley of vision. The rods of chastisement are moments to pause and think. A time that deserves to be remembered, either for the good or the lesson that God was teaching.

Another great Selah time for me was when we opened our new church building. The building program had been a difficult project. There were valleys, deep and long ones, along the way. It was not an easy trip. The day of dedication arrived. I was so obsessed with the goodness of God that I could hardly move. That dedication was special. I felt I would burst. When it was all over, I took a drive. I drove past our other locations and paused to remember. Then I came back up North Cave Creek Road and thought of the groundbreaking, the big hole on the side of the mountain, the day the first struts went up, the generosity of my people, both rich and poor, who placed their funds into our building. I blessed them and thanked them within my heart. And most of all, I thanked God. A cherished moment.

One of my friends and one of our members, Bill Tathum, Jr., had his football team practicing at the high school where we used to have church. I saw them as I drove by. He had been struggling to get his league together. It was a trying time for him. I stopped to write him a letter after that dedication day to let him know that one of these days he would experience what I had on this auspicious occasion. Eventually, for him, things would come together and he too, could look back and know the impossible was accomplished. Because our God is a God of the impossible. In buildings or basketball franchises!

Probably one of my toughest Selahs came at the death of my dad. Now that Dad was with the Lord, I felt an inward poverty. When we used to talk of church needs, developing problems, or even share the big days, Dad had a way of validating me that is not describable. He made me feel like a quarterback hurling the ball to a *known* receiver. Dad was also my wide receiver, my coach, my trainer, and closest friend. If a pass was intercepted and the play failed, as happens in churches, he was there to spark me on with the praise that kept me going . . . ready to pick the ball up again and move on toward the goal line.

Dad was indeed a "known." I knew what to expect from him, and he always came through. In the emptiness of loss, for the first time I wondered if I was now facing God, as a known or barely known person.

What were my inner expectations of God—now that this man I so explicitly trusted was gone?

A major *re-vision* of thinking was forming in my soul. It was not comfortable or explainable. Increasingly I was realizing, as I mentioned previously, that I had built my life and ministry on my father's foundation.

When the call came from Kansas City to our Phoenix home, I responded by taking a walk. It was still dark outside, but the night provided a certain shelter over my grief.

As I walked, I became the architect of a personal, imaginary Hall of Fame, and voted my dad in! I knew he deserved the honor. He had taught me to throw a ball and catch it. He had played with me and supported me in all my events. I hung up pictures of him in my mind and carefully placed them in that Hall of Fame. One was the first sermon I ever preached. He had given me the outline. It was called "The Value of a Soul." I still preach it today.

I hung another developing picture of Dad when he stood with me at our present church location, and heard my vision of the proposed sanctuary to seat seven thousand. It was the last picture my mind had processed. Tears were coming down his cheeks as he gazed at the enormity of our project, and in his quiet fatherly voice said, "Son, you've got a lot of battles ahead of you." I did not know that in just a few days he would die. And his death would become one of my greatest battles—and my ultimate victories.

That long walk down memory lane was a needed catharsis. I was baptized again in Selah.

I went to Dad's funeral in a state of *"thou art."* In a short time I was experiencing, *"thou shalt be."*

If Dad and I could only have talked about the eventuality of his death, possibly I would have been more prepared. God in His wisdom had a better sovereign plan.

The answer to my heart cry, To whom shall I turn? came in perfect stillness one day. "To Me!" Although not audible, I knew it was the voice of the Lord.

Jesus said to Simon, *"Thou art* Simon . . . *Thou shalt be* called Cephas, which is by interpretation, a stone" (John 1:42, emphasis added.)

The Lord was saying to Peter, His disciple, who had a reputation of being quick-tempered as illustrated by the many times that he was in the fire and by the fire, "I am even changing your name. I want to solidify that sandlike nature and make you a rock." *Thou shalt be!* The result—Peter was on fire for the Lord.

The biggest revolution of my life was about to take place. In the past in the areas of prayer and meditation I had struggled. I obeyed with devotions because that was God's command to me. But prayer was not my most earnest desire. When I lost Dad, his strong shoulder and great big heart, I was forced to turn to God with the problems that previously were addressed to my father. Suddenly the Lord and I had an awful lot to talk about! His glorious invitation of "Come to Me, abide with Me, and learn of Me" firsthand was a transforming experience. A conscious awareness of His presence now filled my life. Often I've looked up and hoped Dad knows that none of God's promises he taught to me have failed. They work *first*hand.

"I will say of the Lord, He is my refuge and my fortress, My God, in him will I trust" (Ps. 91:2). I learned that the basis of my security was in the character of Father-God. My line of vision has changed. Now it resembles a straight line joining the fovea of my eye with the fixation point of God's eye. For with David I can say, "My heart is fixed, O God, my heart is fixed" (Ps. 57:7).

I was learning that firsthand revelations from God are the difference between mediocrity and success. A firsthand revelation makes the bitter person better. I discovered that you do not just "take time to be holy," but the people of God must *make* time to be holy. How is that accomplished? Through Selah time.

> Who is this King of glory? The Lord strong and mighty, the Lord mighty in battle. Lift up your heads, O you gates! Lift up, you everlasting doors! and the King of glory shall come in. Who is this King of glory? The Lord of hosts, He is the King of glory. *Selah* (Ps. 24:8-10, emphasis added.)

Selah reminds us who we are and who we are not. It gives us time to know who God is and to rest in Him. The busier I am the more I Selah. I have to because I cannot be everywhere. The church is so vast that it is impossible for me to marry all the people, or bury them, or shake their hands. Therefore I am driven to Selah, and from that time I come forth refreshed and ready to serve them as best I can.

It was after I lost my father that I found what prayer was truly about. Selah became my introduction to prayer time. From there, the prayer overflowed out of my heart. Conversely, I was in-filled from above.

As a result, my ministry changed and the results increased. I had often wondered and prayed in the years that followed my dad's death, that sometime I could see one thousand souls saved on a Sunday morning.

In the summer of 1989, several thousand French people attended a multilevel pyramid-type convention in Phoenix. Leo Godzich and his brother, who is fluent in French, issued invitations to more than four thousand of these European guests to attend our church on a Sunday morning. The necessary arrangements were made and 2,200 attended our service. After presenting the claims of Jesus Christ and extending His invitation "to believe and be saved," more than sixteen hundred responded and stayed for prayer. It was amazing and awesome to see these people, often known for their reserve, come to Jesus. I preached with an interpreter. The Holy Spirit interceded and the kingdom increased.

Some remained in town for weeks, and more than two hundred were baptized before returning to France. "To God be the glory, great things He has done!" Musing for souls in large supply had been a result of Selah time.

Seventy-seven times Scripture displays Selah. More than the term "born again." Its value is priceless. And, as it becomes part of your life, I assure you there will be a major re-vision in your priorities and the results will be awesome.

Selah lifts you from the valley of vision and sets you on a mount of transformation, where His grace and glory are sufficient.

6

Follow Me As
I Follow Christ

I AM surprised at the changing face of the pastor's library. When I was a youngster, I remember being impressed with the books that lined my dad's modest office. They were books about God, commentaries, clips, and articles about people who were making a difference to God. Books are of the utmost importance to me. I love my books and my library. Yet my library focus is singularly unique in that it has few books on leadership, motivation, and guiding staff. Others may pore over what is new in influencing people, the latest books by "hot" authors on motivation, and steps to making people feel important and needed. I am not criticizing, only making an observation.

It may be that this longtime preacher walks to a different beat. I am not saying better, simply a different beat—a heartbeat that says, *Follow me as I follow Christ. The day I do not follow Christ, or make a detour that is not commendable, do not follow me. Help me back on the path of righteousness. If I do not merit your leadership, I will be wise enough to step aside.*

Peter Drucker, that grand old man of corporate wisdom relates—after writing more than twenty books on effective leadership and business management—he can synthesize success in two simple steps:

(1) develop a basic competence and (2) have the will to perform. He is right on!

The apostle Paul wrote this concept into his letters to growing churches and their people.

1. Develop a basic competence? "Let the mind of Christ be in you. Grow in grace in a knowledge of the Lord Jesus Christ. Let the word of Christ dwell in you richly."

Jesus Christ made the ultimate recommendation: "Follow Me and I will *make* you fishers of men."

2. Have the will to perform? Paul wrote the manual: "Being confident of this very thing, that He which hath begun a good work in you will *perform* it until the day of Jesus Christ" (Phil. 1:6, emphasis added).

I believe in leadership by inspiration—not intimidation! When it comes to leadership, I strive to be a "creator" not a "reactor." Creators *act*. Reactors *re-act*. As I follow Christ, I am constantly impressed that He did not just tell His disciples to go and heal the sick and care for the dying. While He was on earth, He did it Himself. As they followed Him, they saw His vision of humanity and were "catching" the concept, so when He went to the Father, they could carry on His works and be commissioned to do even greater works.

In a moment of Selah time I put myself in the sandals of those who were populating the hills of the Holy Land when Jesus first walked among them. It struck me that when He first came to earth, people were disappointed. They had expected to see a king—one who would arrive in regal splendor worthy of a state reception designed for "the greatest of these." After all, the Old Testament stated that the king would come to set up his kingdom. The thought of scepters, a flowing, purple velvet robe, a monarch's traditional diadem, and a military sword surely would accompany him. Celestial choirs and honor guards would delight the people, and first-century versions of the twenty-one-gun salute would reverberate across the hills of Judea.

Instead, He came unrecognized except for angels who sang their own "good tidings of great joy." His earthly parents worshiped God next to the crude cradle in that stable which was His first home. No throngs. No hype. A quiet celebration of heaven, illuminated by a star that flooded the countryside . . . noted only by a handful of wise men and aging prophets.

He arrived as a lowly Savior, this heralded great leader of men. And as He grew, He increased in the wisdom, stature, and innate knowledge of His Father.

The responsibility of raising a "perfect child" surely drew Mary to her share of Selah time. A child who consistently was unique and brilliant. A child she knew was born to be King and her personal Savior.

Suddenly multitudes were "following" Him. Yet He seldom asserted His authority, but presented Himself to the people as a qualified leader. He earned their trust and some "chose" to follow Him.

The basic tenet of my leadership method is *we do not assert ourselves as leaders*—a concept that is seldom practiced. One of the problems in our homes, in our churches, and in our community development is that the wrong kind of assertive leadership may kill the spirit of the people we lead. Blatant "little Caesar" leadership style, saying, "I am the boss—right or wrong—do as I say," takes a high toll in churches as it births an embryo which may grow into discontent, division, and staff departures.

Jesus did not spread the word that He was the King. Even though it was so written. He was earning His title with total commitment and obedience to His Father. He lived the life that spawned followers.

As the leader of a great church, it is surprising to many that I have no official position as pastor of Phoenix First Assembly. I am a board member who has no vote except in the case of a tie. No power except the power of influence . . . but that is all I seek. For I am convinced that unless I influence the board to follow me as I follow the Lord, I have no credentials to lead. *The only power I have is the power I have been given called "followership."*

It is not uncommon to hear ministers quote Hebrews 13:7, 17, "Remember them which have the rule over you. Obey . . . submit yourselves." The author of Hebrews points out that certain types of leadership can be unprofitable. I will not be pastor of my church and lead by assertiveness. My experience says that most assertive leaders want the title and the power. *Earning* leadership is what Jesus did.

True leadership is profiled when the people, by their own actions observe potential and then propel the one in their midst to a position of authority. The leader did not assert himself. He had followed—then the people, seeing his example said they would follow him.

Jesus by now had proven Himself the antithesis of what had been expected. This man from Galilee, and the house of David, acted more like a servant. He had shattered the expected image. The people anticipated a person they would serve and acknowledge as head over all. But Jesus walked as a humble man . . . not a conqueror. He made statements such as, "He that is greatest among you the servant shall be."

From observation and study, I have found there are three kinds of leaders. Their qualities were well described by Dr. Jack Hyles. The first portrait of a leader is a person who has *strength that others do not have*. His strength may be drawn upon without depleting the supply. This person possesses an "excess" that is uncommon, and so is elevated to leadership. History presents people like this such as the Caesars, the Charlemagnes, or a Sampson—men who have possessed herculean strength, although it was not always used for good. Women have not been exempt.

The next aspect of a leader would be one who possesses *truth that others do not possess*, as illustrated by a Plato or Aristotle. These people were rarely strong physically, but their knowledge and rare ability set them apart. Through them, others were taught, and the teachers became leaders.

The third form of leadership exists in men who have a *holiness that others do not possess*. A consuming thirst to know the Lord. A burning desire to do the will of the Father. George Mueller was such a man of faith. We know he did not excel in strength, but his source of truth was Scripture. He practiced "Be ye holy as I am holy." He was forced into leadership as he followed God. He had such a life that his "excess" was the means of others gaining strength, grasping truth, and seeking holiness.

My heroes are men who possess Mr. Mueller's traits. He prayed down the power and the provision for his orphanage. His story is legendary and his "excesses" of God became a reservoir of faith for God's people the world over.

Consider the Andrew Murrays, the Mother Teresas, or a man like Dr. Mark Buntain, who was recently graduated to glory. They symbolize stalwarts of the faith, and their works will follow them. Each would say, *only* follow me as I follow Christ. Each possessed the qualities of self-effacement and a ready-to-sacrifice-all attitude that caused others to go and do likewise.

We need a fresh portion of the holiness of God. The kind that leads to purity and devotion. A person of holiness makes those around desire the same, and like a great magnetic force for good, the willing learner leaves with a taste of new strength, knowledge, and holiness, drawn from the well of one of God's great, resolute servants.

I like the kind of leadership that combines the first two qualities but emphasizes the latter. *The holiness.* This kind of leadership models part hero, part teacher, and lots of saint! Why is this vital to a church body? Because everyone in God's family has the potential of leadership. Some lead homes, others businesses, some lead ministries. We must be developing people for God's glory and His service. My church is made up of ministers and ministers-to-be. In another chapter I will share how I treat and feed my flock—just like a Pastors' School. Then all my people leave the services as ministers to go forth and minister to the needs of a dying world.

If we are to be leaders, it must be not just because we are elected. We have too much of that in this world. There are a lot of elected politicians who have trouble leading their own families. Some I know personally.

After a visit to the White House, I came away amazed, not that so little is accomplished, but that anything is accomplished at all. I love the White House. I support everything for which it stands. But I was discouraged by the conflict and confusion and mountains of paper that bury the treasure of people's creativity. I longed to see some qualities of great leadership at the center of this incredible nation. I said to one of our national leaders, "I wish I could bring this bunch to Pastors' School."

In World War II most of the officers were trained at OCS. However, on the battlefield, as the officers were killed, enlisted men rose up on their own, and their men pronounced them leaders. Why? Because in daily living they had exemplified those qualities of strength, knowledge, and wholeness. History relates that many of these men were the ones who orchestrated the winning campaigns and encounters of that war.

Candidates are not leaders just because they get votes. Perhaps the campaign manager had the charisma and the advertising agency the right stuff, and the candidate became secondary to the strategy of the writers, movers, and shakers. The most votes garnered is not necessarily indicative of the best official.

What the world is crying for is leaders with the right "excess." As we move toward the twenty-first century, the church should provide the kind of leadership that is shaping other leaders. Futurists are saying there is little hope of America's competing in the future, let alone surviving. In only a few short years our beloved country has moved from being the world's largest creditor nation to becoming the world's greatest debtor nation. Economists remind us that once we were the ultimate in producing scientists and high technology. Now our high tech is used to measure trade deficits.

As a pastor I am very concerned with the "gross national fear" that grips the world. Fear for the multitudes who have never heard the message *fear not*. America was founded as a Christian nation. We need to produce the leadership that alleviates that gross national fear and transforms it, through the power of God, into "gross national profit" for our Lord.

Jesus was the epitome of "excess." He went around, moved with compassion for the multitude. He gave me the desire to *count people because people count*. The great multitudes that followed Him were aware of His strength. The response was, "We want that." He spoke the truth as One with authority. They responded, "We want that." They saw His holiness and said, "We want to get close to Him!" So they kept on following Him wherever He went. These are the qualities that attracted people to Jesus.

Notice here we have a hero. One who has made it possible to give of His strength—strength that has proven to be made "perfect in weakness." The kind of strength children felt when they were around Jesus, for His strength emanated from His Father's heart of love. Physical strength that could be derived by the ill and infirm who came for healing.

Many of us have people close to us who are sources of strength. A mom or a dad or family member. Sometimes people are blessed with strong employers who are fair and share themselves. However, we must be alert to see the many who have *no* arm to lean upon. So those of us who are strong need to bear the infirmities of the weak. And become a hero to those who have none.

A leader needs to keep bringing truth to his people. He must work for new understanding and resources. He must research and learn what is going on in his city and world, so he is a source of relating the gospel to issues and needs. He lifts his cup so it is constantly filled from the storehouse of the Lord.

So what does he do? When he is drained, he goes to the real well—the Master's source, and drinks freely of the river of life; he returns again and again for more heavenly watering power. This comes only from prayer, from the Word, and becoming insatiable searchers for truth.

That is why I spend at least two hours on the mountain every morning. Even the mornings following a major church event when I helped remove props until 2 A.M., I go to the mountain to keep my unbreakable appointment with my Father. It is not a debatable appointment, but is chiseled on the tablet of my heart—decreed through my intellect, my volition, and my affection for Father-God that

> I will lift up my eyes to the mountains;
> From whence shall my help come?
> My help comes from the Lord,
> —Psalm 121: 1, 2

What more solid appointment could be made and kept than with the One who is the source of these promises? Our Creator who does not slumber nor sleep. God is never unmindful of His very own.

Mountains have a way of bringing us down to size with the reminder: "What is man that Thou art mindful of him?" If a sparrow falls and He notices, I know He is mindful of me!

Most mornings I get up early and take my coffee up to the side of the mountain behind our church. I don't always talk when I pray. I have relished the times of just *being with* God, being open to His Spirit and enjoying His company. Two hours is no magic formula, but it is a space of time I deeply appreciate, and a time I seek to develop those qualities

I need to lead God's people. This is also a time when I can share my dreams with the Lord. My thoughts can run rampant in that secret place where no one will laugh at the impossibility of some of my future plans. I find as I seek to live in the will of God, my dreams are His dreams, and He has the capacity to make those dreams come true.

The Holy Spirit becomes my prayer partner. As the firsthand revelations unfold from God, the Holy Spirit is there, real, in person, inspiring my heart, praying with me and encouraging my dreams—just like my dad used to do.

The children of Israel found that it was a simple matter to let Moses go up to Mount Sinai and talk to the Lord for them. They did not have to take the time or expend the energy for a firsthand encounter with God.

God wants to speak directly. Everyone must spend time on the mountain themselves. The visions and plans He has for me are right for me, and the experience He has for each individual is also perfect. Never doubt that! Time on the mountain with the Lord, and lots of intervals in between, are the foundation for joy and strength each day. It has been said that if you fill your cup up to the brim with the Lord, then whatever else goes into the cup will make it overflow!

If the full cup has a disappointment drop in, it still overflows. If an unexpected surprise arrives, airmail from heaven, that causes an overflow, too. Whichever way, keep the cup full of the Lord. Then you can say with David, "My cup runneth over!" And over again!

When services are over on Sunday night, I go home and often run for several miles. I usually listen to a tape of the Word of God or to a great preacher or teacher. All week I consciously seek to fill my life with godly input. In the car I hear the word on the tape deck. Sometimes good gospel music enriches my soul. There are even times I take a book to the mountain. My staff and people can discern the time I spend on that mountain. It reappears in my preaching.

I had the false impression, when I was a young preacher, that the day would come when I could begin to relax in my study. Have more free time. See more things. It was logical, I thought, that after several years of preparing messages, a formula would make it easier. Also, I could call up previous things from a backlog of subjects, or warm over old messages with contemporary illustrations.

Just the opposite has proved to be true. I find the older I get, the more I have to depend on God. The more I seek His face. The more prayer I require. Charles Wesley wrote that "nothing is accomplished except by prayer." I believe now more than ever that his statement is true. The blessing of God in our lives is predicated on the time we spend with Him. I know the more I pray, the more power. The more I study, the more powerful the message to penetrate people's lives. The more I thank God for mercy, the more tears I shed. The more I say, "Fill me," the more filling I desire.

At Phoenix First Assembly we have had some great people on our platform. How I thank God for them and for their influence. We have witnessed great leadership in many churches. We want to keep ourselves in a learning mode from people, but it is God who ripens the fruit of a prepared heart.

I thank God for the people who stand with me in my church. How I love and appreciate them. They came up through the church's ranks. Many started as volunteers and kept working for God. Most were not leaders of organizations or churches before they came here. They rose to their place of leadership because those around them "lifted them on their shoulders" in response to their excess of strength, knowledge, and holiness. They attracted others to drink, and they refused to run dry.

Carmen Balsamo, a wonderful man, is with the Lord now, but I recall the first time I met him. Larry Kerychuk was discipling him. Carmen did not attend this church. Larry poured the Word of God into Carmen along with prayer and himself. One day Carmen got a hold of the secrets of Larry's excesses and became a man who started pouring himself into others. He was filled with the holiness of God. He was not a great preacher, or an outstanding scholar, but young people loved him and found a person they could draw from. The Master's Commission people found a friend and ally, but most of all, a qualified leader they could trust. Carmen's influence stretched around our campus like a dose of good deeds and bundles of encouragement.

When I was twenty-three years old, I met Mark Buntain in India. He has been called "Saint Mark of Calcutta." The compassion of this man was a story—for books and dramas and articles. But how he walked with God has never been told.

I will never forget the day he said to me, "Tommy, you have to pray for me today. I am exhausted. People do not think I can carry on. The load is unbearable. I feel as if there is a band around my head. Pray for me, because I know if I go home, they will not let me come back, and there is no one to take my place. I have to stay here."

My mind was torn about that prayer. What would be best for the man of God? A rest or a breakdown? It should not have been an issue, but I felt led to pray for his restoration. Years later in his book, *St. Mark of Calcutta,* he related the significance of that prayer and how God had restored him right in the middle of traffic. He stayed in India.

In Mark Buntain I saw a man I wanted to follow. In him I saw strength even in weakness. I saw his skill and knowledge and watched him use it and extend it in every possible, difficult way. I saw holiness—the kind I wanted to ascribe to. And the fruit of that holiness in his daily life. He was what he was, *not* because he was assertive. He was not. He lacked what some call charisma. However, the glory of God was all over that man, and his work touched nerve centers of India. This godly, kind, gentle leader may be looking down at India from the heavenly streets of gold. What does he see in 1989?

A thousand national leaders that he "inspirationally" trained. Thirteen thousand children in school—kindergarten through junior high—within twelve schools he built. Thirty thousand nursing mothers and children, fed every day in Calcutta. Seventy preaching points, rural and urban, where scores hear of Jesus Christ. (Mark and his wife Huldah built the first church in Calcutta to be erected in over one hundred years. It serves eight languages! And in his death, his wife continues to administrate and encourage his vision of a new church that is now planned.) Mark built a one-hundred-sixty-bed hospital, manned by forty doctors, and established rural clinics and MASH-style ambulances for places where there are no hospitals.

It all started when he saw a tiny child who had not eaten for three days. He saw a need. He met it. He discovered millions of hurts and healed them with his compassionate touch and cross-shaped heart. Another man of God, like my father, who overdosed on life.

I interviewed Dr. Bill Bright of Campus Crusade for Christ. As I listened to this humble, down-to-earth man, he reminded me a lot of my dad. I started following Bill in my heart. This man has never accepted an offering in his life. He has no last will and testament for anyone except his ministry. In him I saw strength and knowledge and holiness. His people follow him as he follows Christ.

Talk with leaders, and generally you will learn that they were often chosen by "followers," and now carry the load because leadership qualifications emerged. They did not conquer their followers. Their followers conquered them.

Dr. George Truett was a pastor for forty years. He founded the First Baptist Church in Dallas, Texas, still one of the great churches of our time. He was a layman in a country church when the pastor resigned. When the people asked him to pastor them, he said he did not feel called. He didn't believe he could do it. They countered by telling him that *they* felt led for him to come. It was his "excesses" that attracted those people to him. He accepted *their* call and his ministry accomplishments entered the annals of church history.

Burdens and calls are different things. It is easy to get a burden for something when you see a need—a hungry child in a country of famine. You send a check for a few months and the burden is dropped. However, when a call of God comes, the Bible says it is without repentance.

I had no burden to come to Phoenix First Assembly. My burden was Davenport, Iowa. The Sunday I rolled into town and walked onto the platform, I had no burden for this church. I was a pastor with no burden, but a definite call. Two weeks later as I drove down the streets of Phoenix, I was touched by the kids in the inner city, which no one was reaching. Now I doubt there is a pastor in America who has a greater burden for his church than I do for mine.

As I look at the individuals who have influenced my life, I believe that Dale Carnegie would never have chosen them as motivators. However, they were chosen of God and have been found obedient. *People who walk behind them will find them faithful.* These leadership qualities are qualities we each may possess. I have heard people say they want these qualities, not to be leaders but to help people. Having a strength that others do not have, a truth that others do not have, and a holiness that others do not seek, combined with an excess of them all are the criteria on which others can draw.

Over the years I have set out to find the common denominator of all the great people in the land who were serving God. I also wanted to find it in warriors of the faith who have gone before. I read biographies, made copious notes, looked for similarities, and sought for differences. It has been a long struggle. I was amazed that some of the greats preached only twenty minutes, some an hour and a half. The length of the sermon was not a criterion. I looked at their education. D. L. Moody lacked a high school diploma, but R. A. Torry was a known and respected scholar. Billy Sunday preached with notes that were enlarged so he could see them as he would run by during his sermon, breaking chairs and trying to race across the platform as though he were sliding into second base!

Jonathan Edwards read his great sermons word for word. His completed works are volumes long. And it was purported that he did not even read well.

I found that education, sermon length, dynamic delivery and appearance had nothing to do with their profession or performance for Christ. Cultural backgrounds were just as diversified. But what I did learn was that each one had a very specific call. Each one had an all-encompassing *burden for lost souls*. All had the ability to face difficult situations because they interfaced passionately with God and carried the marks of a leader.

Jonathan Edwards, called the last of the Puritans, was not only a great preacher and prolific writer, but a graduate of Yale University and a president of Princeton. While pastoring a great church, one of his members began competing with him. In time the jealous parishioner spread lies about Dr. Edwards that were published in the *Boston Globe*. The pastor was forced out of his church. In the interim his family of nine children was ostracized by the public—other children would not even speak to his young ones. They moved to a tiny, rural church, where for ten years they lived, victims of vicious lies.

Not once did Dr. Edwards fight back. During the long exile he produced great books, including some of the greatest books on theology to this time. Here was a man of great strength, enormous knowledge, and personal holiness who was opposed *not* by ungodly people, but by Christians. During the turbulence they maintained forgiving spirits, and although truth ultimately prevailed, he was an old man when justice was served.

Some would say, "How tragic. What purpose this waste?" Jonathan and Sarah Edwards would respond that the purposes of God were still carried out in their lives, for their calls to personal holiness exceeded the slander and pain imposed on them.

> Blessed are ye, when men shall revile you and persecute you, and shall say all manner of evil against you falsely, for my sake. Rejoice and be exceeding glad: for great is your reward in heaven: for so persecuted they the prophets which were before you. (Matt. 5:11-12)

Leadership has its deep trials and times of failure and defeat. One "called" does not turn back when the call is deposited in the Lord's treasury. As a pastor's son, raised in an Assembly of God home, I watched people misuse the power of the Holy Spirit. I had been taught all my life that when you receive the power of the Holy Spirit, it gives you power to witness. And yet some who spoke in tongues were among the worst witnesses I knew, while some who did not speak in tongues were among the greatest.

I had been taught that the Holy Spirit made you live a holy life. I worked with people lacking that persuasion whose lives were holier.

I had been told that the Holy Spirit was a great comforter, yet I had noticed that some of the people who gave my dad the worst time in the church were those who spoke in tongues. And some of our sweetest friends did not.

You can see why I was in a maelstrom of confusion. I searched a long time for answers.

I was getting ready to build a church. I wanted to do it like Jesus did. So I started asking questions about the Holy Spirit. I started to circle the continents to talk to people and great men who built churches. I learned the Holy Spirit is our comforter. I discovered He is a gentleman. I found out that when the Spirit of God moves, it is with decency and order. I found the gifts of the Holy Spirit are operated by the Holy Spirit, and I came to the life-changing conclusion that the Holy Spirit is not just an experience, but is truly a person.

If you want to be a leader you must earn that leadership. Never be assertive. You must abide in the Book and search to know God.

When the sun rises on the mountain by our church, I see scores of people of all races, from all backgrounds, seeking the face of God.

Some walk and pray. Some kneel in reverence before God. Some weep and smile in His presence. These are the people I believe are God's "remnant" people. Pillars of the church, sanctified, and set apart for His work.

They have discovered the "secret place of the Most High" and abide "under the shadow of His wings." From their time on the mountain, they will go down and take the cross into the streets. As they work, many will be lifted up on the shoulders of those around them and be commissioned as leaders—possessing the qualifications of great strength, knowledge, and visible holiness. What a treasure for God!

What a responsibility for their pastor. For these are the ones who follow me as I follow God.

7

Jesus Never Forgets

"The steps of a good man are ordered by the Lord, and he delights in his way. *Though he fall, he shall not be utterly cast down;* for the Lord upholds him with His hand" (Ps. 37:23, 24, emphasis added).

A PASTOR can ask no greater affirmation from his church than to be granted the possibility to fail. Mine have given that to me with love. However, they are not into allowing me to fail *on the same matter* for a second time!

God is a God of everything but failure! We often say He can do everything but fail. Jesus never fails! But the reality of life is this—there are times we fail.

Jesus predicted failure. That is why graciously He responds that "though he fall, he shall not be utterly cast down: for the Lord upholdeth him with His hand!" There is not a lot that separates failure and success. Talk with athletes. The winning edge may be gained by a thousandth of a second. Or an almost indiscernable move, to the non-professional spectator, which makes the winning difference.

Talk with Mark Spitz, the five-time Olympic gold medal winner in swimming. It appeared in his prime that everything he touched turned to gold. His defeated teammate said, "Everything I touch these days, I have to put back!" Vince Lombardi, the fabled coach, wrote his belief across the performance of his players: "Winning isn't everything, it is the *only* thing." Yet what happens when athletes or pastors give their best performance, and it proves to be a disappointment?

In our Pastors' School stories of failure supersede those of success. One man, broken from the inside out, confessed he had done his best, yet he felt invalidated. He had tried and tried to build his church and encourage his people, and the effort merited the same empty seats. He was encouraged by one of my associates who reminded him that if he does not try he will not fail. For *true failure is in not trying.* Winning, in God's way, comes from faithfulness, obedience, and courage to keep going.

Winning has a double edge. Winning can be winning or winning can be losing. This is a *re-vision* in most of our thinking today. Some of us remember one of the national finals of the Special Olympics. Our hearts are tugged by those loving and courageous kids—kids who nudge the tender places and have a way of tapping on the walls of our deepest emotions. (Some of them remind me a lot of the bus kids who call Phoenix First their home.)

The event was the difficult 440-yard dash. A young, mentally retarded boy led the field all the way from the starting gun into the homestretch. Suddenly, he collapsed with muscle spasms and cramps. As the second- and third-place runners drew alongside, they could have pulled ahead for the gold and silver. Instead they stopped and picked up the fallen competitor. With his arms around their shoulders, they finished the last ten yards and broke the tape *together.* The people cheered! Everyone won. No one lost!

I saw a living, breathing example of the Bible truth that states, "We who are strong ought to bear with the failings of the weak and not just please ourselves. Each of us should please his neighbor for his good, to build him up" (Rom. 15:1-2 NIV.)

The double side of winning was also seen in Calgary one year through the speed-skating scenario of Dan Jansen. Portraits of him and his large family had been painted in contrasting colors throughout the various media. The fact that his sister was dying, and she treasured his quest for gold, became a household story.

Dan tried twice, and he fell twice. He failed twice. Most Americans shared the painful moments. But Dan did not lose in his game plan of life. For he picked himself up and went on, two weeks later, to capture the gold in the world championship. The newspapers headlined, "Here is a Three-time Winner!" Once in his event. Twice in life.

Pastors and ministering people have a lot in common with athletes, for we all create our own brand of hopes and dreams and visions. Most of us know what it is like to fall and get hurt. Sometimes our feelings hurt most, but we must expect failure as part of the journey. What is important is our relationship to that failure.

God's children possess an edge that the world does not claim. "Nay, in all these things we are *more than conquerors* through Him that loved us" (Rom. 8:37). We are not just garden-variety conquerors but *more than* conquerors. That gives us courage to move ahead. Few have learned to give themselves enough credit for falls or failures. Just about everything in life includes losing. Experiencing rejection, filing for a Chapter Eleven bankruptcy, missing a Sunday school goal, letting sin gain an upper edge, crowding out devotions and Selah time—all stockpiles of failures that *may* become foundations upon which you can build and rebuild. Enjoying success and facing failure both have a way of teaching us to overcome the fear of both.

Victory in the dark experiences of life is to affirm and proclaim our wholeness in Christ. People say to me, "Pastor, you just don't know what it is to have your dream collapse all over the floor. Things have gone easy for you." I am torn by those comments as to the best way to respond. Easy? Never! I have had my share of shattered dreams and basketsful of a broken heart. God never promised complete success. He promised victory even in the dark experiences of life. I have been successful in knowing that my plans and my thoughts have *not* always been in His time interval (Selah hindsight!). "For My thoughts are not your thoughts, Neither are your ways My ways . . . for as the heavens are higher than the earth, so are My ways higher than your ways, and My thoughts than your thoughts" (excerpts from Isa. 55:8-9). I must learn the lesson of "bringing into captivity every thought to the obedience of Christ" (2 Cor. 10:5).

Part of my dream since coming to Phoenix was to build a modest little prayer chapel halfway up the mountain. It would be placed in a wonderful, natural garden. The cacti would be in place, and the local habitat would be honored. This chapel would be for God's glory, and a symbol to the community that people are praying twenty-four hours a day on that mountain. The Shadow Mountains afforded us the opportunity of literally living in the *shadow* of the Almighty.

I felt hope would swell up in needy people who drove by, saw the chapel with its cross, and know in their beings that this chapel was representative of God. Here I envisioned twelve telephone lines in a soundproofed room that would be manned without interruption, where people could answer the needs of people who sought counsel or prayer, people who were on the verge of suicide, who may have lost a loved one and did not know how to cope. There are drug overdoses and emotional disorders that fall heavy on Phoenix. Our present hotlines were overcrowded, and we needed a new location.

For years I had shared my dream with the congregation. They were excited. Many had already supported it financially. God's people support a vision that reaches beyond the church's front door. This vision had far-reaching implications.

I knew this was of God just because of the solemnity of the program. It was for His glory. I would be amazed at the extra gifts of money slipped into my hand for "Prayer Mountain" from the rich and from the needy. One woman brought a large portion of her meager welfare check. Her note was written in stumbling English but the content triggered my heart and had to touch God's. She gave us a piece of paper that said, "Poor as this offering may be, it is my very best ever gift to the Lord. More than everything I have ever given to anyone that ever lived. This is for Mount Prayer!"

This poor woman had given it her all. She may have been the face of poverty, but in my mind she stood for wealth, and I know her gift in the sight of God stood proudly beside the widow's mite.

Yet something, somewhere, went wrong. The city wrote us a letter to say they were condemning eleven acres on that side of the mountain, and they were going to make it a mountain preserve. Eleven acres that were our acres.

I talked to God. I shared with the lawyers and my godly advisers to see what we should do. I felt like my heart had fled from my chest and had fallen on the hard rocks. Encouragement came when a council person asked me to speak, and explain what we were going to do. I accepted the invitation, and went down to share my dream—a dream that would be valid for the city as well, for through that chapel's crises lines, hungry people would be fed, poor people clothed, and hurting people helped.

The next day the newspaper fabricated a story announcing that the church was going to build a seventy-foot prayer tower on the side of Shadow Mountain! The article stated we were planning to deface the mountain. The paper compared our tiny house of help to Oral Roberts's towering prayer structure. But we had not planned any kind of a spire. Just a simple cross in keeping with the landscape and the chapel, built by the side of the hill. A truly humble place.

I was quick to call the newspapers and the environmentalists and explain that there was to be no giant spire. They had published facts that were wrong and deceptive. They refused to refute the story or to print my true blueprint for the chapel. I was crushed, hurt, and angry. I called the editor again and asked for an interview. It was coldly denied. He said that he would do exactly what he wanted to do and print what he wanted to print. I knew then, I was headed for trouble.

Next the papers started carrying cartoons. One was a cartoon in the shape of a crown. The crown formed a distorted prayer chapel. On top of the crown was a spire, and topping off the spire were dollar signs. The caption was the greatest heartbreak of all: *"First Assembly of Tommy Barnett!"* I felt trapped between a rock and a hard place. Had it not been for the love of my people and the grace of God, I would not have been able to accept the comforting truth of God's Word: "When my heart is overwhelmed, lead me to the Rock that is higher than I." The Rock that is higher than my dream or hope or expectation. Surely our Gibraltar—Rock of Ages—was sovereignly aware of the inaneness of an unfair press, and the results of the "council of the ungodly."

If there is anything I dislike, it is a person who steps in front of God's glory. I preach from the pulpit that God will destroy anything that takes away from Him. We use our many buildings for people. My office, furnished and designed in southwestern style, houses a Sunday school class and midweek missionettes. Nothing is kept from God's use. Nothing that we have ever built has been a monument to people. I have never been a caretaker to a building. Everything in our church is for God's use. Everything is dedicated to Him.

The next cartoon was Tommy Barnett in a loud, ugly jacket with a big Bible under his arm. The Bible had a TV on the front of it. In the background was a bulldozer tearing down a cactus . . . cactus carefully protected in Arizona.

Those who know me know how conservative I am in dress and manner. They also know that I personally implement Psalm 24:1, "The earth is the Lord's and all its furnishings." Cactus and mountains are part of God's magnificent furnishings. Our church has received impressive awards for commercial landscaping.

The last cartoon was run the day before the city council would vote as to whether we could have our seventeen hundred square foot chapel. This cartoon was set in South Dakota, where the four presidents are carved into the Black Hills. To the presidents they had added my face. The caption read: "Barnett Mountain!" I was completely speechless and flabbergasted. We had worked on making known our position. It had been ignored. Again the newspaper had chosen to do as it pleased.

When I went down to the council meeting, the press was there, and the cameras were rolling. I asked to speak before the council before the vote and was granted a hearing. I said that I was sorry if we had caused the city any hurt. We never had the intention of hurting or marking the mountain in any way. Our motive was to build a small prayer chapel, which would house the crisis lines to do one thing—help humankind. However, due to the newspaper's false impressions, we were withdrawing our request immediately. I said that we would not build that chapel if someone gave us a million dollars. We had desired to help the city because we believe the church should assume a great part of the burden for hurting people. The burden should not rest on the government alone.

I then turned to the mountain preserve crowd and officials and addressed them. I stated that one thing would be appreciated. The next time they wanted property that belonged to the church, my board and I would be grateful if we were extended the courtesy of their coming to us first. We were the last to know they had such intentions. The newspaper was no place to carry on such an underhanded campaign. It was heartbreaking that people said we were going to deface the mountains, and then try to destroy our testimony and the good that was being done, as a means of winning their case. I explained we were reasonable people and always willing to talk—but not through the cartoon sketches.

I left the council chambers. I was later told that the mayor came down on the press for their irresponsible actions. It was too late.

I have never been one to go on talk shows, but I felt this time that I should champion truth. The first host who contacted me stated on the air that "Public opinion is surely against you, isn't it?" My response was that I was not that sure the newspapers spoke for all the people. Why did we not have people call in? (My church did not even know I was on the talk show so there was no way the calls could be rigged.) The host agreed. Much to his amazement, everyone but one of the callers was *for* us. The next day I went on another show. The same thing was true. The host gave three hours for people to call in, and the response was the greatest in the history of the station. The results: 76 percent for us, 24 percent against. I went on the third talk show, and received another overwhelming response, with the figures weighted even more heavily in our favor.

Much of the underlying problem of the chapel controversy had to do with the stories of the fallen Christian leaders. It appeared that it was "open season" on the church. We were one of the many casualties. The newspapers had become the spokespeople. They are held accountable. We got a bad rap. However, we serve a sovereign God, and I still believe His purpose will be accomplished.

Why? Because Jesus never fails! Men may foil the plans but God triumphs. Never had Jeremiah 29:11 been more significant: "For I know the plans I have for you, declares the Lord, plans to prosper you and not to harm you, plans to give you hope and a future" (NIV).

I remembered the story of Dwight L. Moody, who looked at the ashes of the great Chicago fire and saw a Bible Institute, a place to train missionaries and pastors and publish books and do good. His struggles to achieve that goal made my disappointment come into perspective. But the fact of history is, Moody's vision stands today as a great asset to the work of the Lord and science.

My dream did not die in the arms of those environmentalists and people who accepted Satan's lies. It is still very much alive. I may have to transfer the vision to another location or go through a lot of *re-vision*, but our chapel will someday, for God's glory, be a reality.

The reason that I am sure that God will gain the ultimate glory in the prayer chapel comes from an encounter I had with another city council.

We are our experience. God has His way of preparing us for what will cross our paths. After all, He sees the end from the beginning.

One afternoon I was taking my young son to get a haircut. In the barber shop he picked up a magazine. As he looked at it, I realized it was nothing but hard-core pornography. I made a trip to the grocery store to purchase some flour. Again I noticed that the magazine section was lined with more pornography. Something within me welled up and said this was not right. People should have the choice to go to the barber or the grocery store without it resembling an X-rated bookstore. I was incensed.

The next Sunday morning I told my congregation what I had seen, and I said to them they all must come Sunday night. By the help and grace of God, we were going to turn things around in our city. Well, the word spread. The newspapers came. The television cameras were present. The place was packed out. I preached a sermon called, "We Want Our Rights."

I explained that this was a day when women wanted rights, when minorities wanted rights, when gays wanted rights. Everyone wants their rights. I believed there was a group who were not getting their "rights," and that was the church of Jesus Christ. I felt it was a *right* of Christians to go to a barber shop or grocery store and not be subjected to illicit print media. After they applauded, I told them what I felt God would want us to do.

Each one, if they agreed was to go to the places where they traded, and if those books or magazines were displayed, they were to say, "Mr. Proprietor, I love to come to this store. I have traded here for years. I want to continue to trade here, but I cannot with conscience bring my children here. In the next few weeks, if these items are not removed or relocated from sight, I will have to go to a place that caters to my kind of clientele." I explained that we must be gracious. We must be kind. We are Christians. But the time had come to be firm. Then I told them to explain that the pastor is making a list of the places that will comply with our concerns, and it will be charted on the back wall of the church.

The next day the headlines reported, "Barnett Declares War On Pornography." And we did. In the following weeks our people went to stores and, of the five major grocery chains, all complied with our wishes. Either the books in question were taken from the shelves completely, or they were placed behind counters where customers would have to ask. Other churches joined us, Protestant and Catholic. The people united in a good spirit of wanting their rights. It was a victory.

Then our young people came to me and said that they wanted permission to go down to the areas where the massage parlor and adult bookstores were. They wanted to start witnessing and attempt to shut those places down. My young people were fired up with our victory. They wanted to advance some more. *Say a good Amen!*

I went to the county attorney and asked him if it was legal for our kids to do that. He said it definitely was and gave us permission. So the kids went for many months, even in the cold winter, sometimes just to hand out tracts. People would be making their way into the bookstore or massage parlor, and the kids would give them a tract and tell them that God loved them. Frequently, the person would just walk on by.

It was not long until business was failing for those merchants. The economic pinch was obvious. People were just embarrassed to be seen going in.

One of the young men came to me, delighted with his news that only one person had gone into the massage parlor he had been assigned to for that day. He explained that he had developed a new system. He had found an old camera that did not work, and when people turned into those establishments, he pretended to snap a picture. They were unaware that the camera was broken!

One day another of these young men was handing a tract to a man who was a prospective patron. The man was told that Jesus loved him, and with that news, he hauled off and hit the church person right in the mouth, knocking him down. The Christian stood up, spit out the blood, and said to him, "Mister, Jesus still loves you."

The man went home and could not sleep. He kept remembering the bloody kid saying, "Jesus still loves you." The next Wednesday night he came to Westside Assembly's prayer meeting and came to the front. He told us what had happened, and the fact that all he could see since that event was the boy who said, "Jesus loves you." He related that as a child he had gone to church with his mother and had become a member of a Baptist church. His life was tremendously turned around.

The young people continued their quest. In the midst of the battle the police came to them and told them if they did not get off the street they would be put in jail. They told the officer that their pastor had gotten permission from the city attorney, who had said it was legal.

The kids called the church. They wanted permission to stay on the street. I told them they had my permission to continue their morality patrol. The next call came from the city jail. They had been arrested and all nine of them jailed.

I rushed to the jail, and found an officer with his feet on the desk. He acted irritated. I told him he was in trouble because my kids had had permission from the city attorney, and they had been stopped, arrested, and put in jail. At that moment the telephone rang. The officer was looking worried. He hung up the phone and talked to me with a concerned-sounding voice. He admitted he was in trouble—for since the nine young people had been jailed, thirty-six more kids had already replaced them.

I looked at him, and said that by tomorrow night when I would tell my congregation about this, I envisioned thirteen hundred moms and dads and other people would be joining the thirty-six! There was a long pause. He stood up and said, "If you will get those people off the street, tomorrow I will help you develop an ordinance against those bookstores and parlors." I agreed.

The next morning the headlines blared, "Police Arrest the Westside Nine!" It was like we had another Chicago Seven. The story related that Pastor Barnett had said if the city did not change their ordinance, he would block every evil door with people lending their support to the proposed new ordinance.

The city fathers went to work! Within three weeks they passed an ordinance that literally shut down those places. The newspapers were for us. The press was good. Very different from the prayer chapel press we received in Phoenix.

The papers printed a wonderful story lauding our people for the job they had done. One paper said that "It is time instead of throwing kids in jail, they should award them a medal for doing what the city fathers did not have the courage to do. It is time we turn such major projects as the beautification of the riverfront to Westside Assembly of God church. They know how to get things done!"

But the battle was not over. The massage parlors were owned by perceived underworld crime figures. All of a sudden I was getting letters and phone calls threatening to blow up my church and shoot me as I stood in the pulpit. We got through the first month of threats. Next they were going to kill my children. We got through the next month.

In the interim, two men were brought in from Detroit and Toledo as reinforcements for the massage parlors. One of the female owners said the face of one of those men was more sinister than anything she had encountered. That owner came to us and was gloriously saved. Later on, four of the six owners found Christ.

As the death threats continued, we put our children in a country school where we felt they would be safe. We all were living close to God because the intimidation did not cease. Then a letter arrived threatening to take my wife if I did not pull back from the campaign against the massage parlors and adult bookstores. Included in the letter were pictures—filthy pictures—of what they would do to Marja. Although it might have been another scare tactic, we took careful precautions. At night the police helicopter flew over our home. We had a wire crossing the doorways to alert us if anyone came in. We stayed upstairs, fearful of firebombing.

In Pennsylvania my preaching was interrupted by a call from my dear wife. Marja was crying. A neighbor had noticed that someone had been watching her with binoculars. As she was driving home, he chased her in his car. She had only recently learned to drive. He pulled beside her, forcing her to the side of the road. She jumped out of the car and ran into a farmhouse, with the man in pursuit. As she outran him and dashed through the door, she was met by a woman, angry about her intrusion. Marja explained that she was being chased. The lady of the house was stunned. She explained that only moments before she had gone to that very door—locked it, chained it, and *bolted* it shut. There was no way Marja could have come through that door. But she did! Without a mark on her. God had gone before and behind her! *He* is ultimate security.

The massage parlors sent a lawyer to sue us for my shutting them down. The lawyer was saved in our church and became our church attorney. One of the girls who had owned one of the parlors found Christ and subsequently married a professor. She called recently to reaffirm her walk with the Lord.

The incidents surrounding those days made headlines and national news. Television networks told of what was happening in Davenport, Iowa. CBN stood with us in reporting the progress. Christians supported us with prayer. A local resident had a tee shirt imprinted "Barnett is a Turkey. We have a right to choose." One of my young men countered with his own version: "Barnett may be a Turkey, but he certainly is NO Chicken." During those days public opinion was on our side. The mayor was converted. Senator Roger Jepson found Christ. After that he would not campaign on Sunday.

To date the ordinance stands!

When I left to come to Arizona, I was given the key to the city. I received a Man of the Year award. The newspapers in that area still carry what happens to us in this church, and always in a sense of goodwill and concern.

One of the last articles I read from Davenport was one that carried the negative outcome of the prayer chapel. The friendly Iowa press ended their story by saying that they were sure that the issue is not closed. And if they were betting on anyone, they would be betting on Tommy Barnett!

I interpreted their statement believing they meant to say they were betting on God!

When visions and dreams like the prayer chapel are stopped, it is innate in people to say, Why dream any more? It is more likely than not most visions are squelched somewhere along the line. I do not adhere to that reasoning. The Bible is full of dreamers and visionaries—people who saw beyond their physical sight, looked into the distances of God, and saw what breaks His heart.

I am reminded of Joseph. In fact his family used to say with a snarl, "There goes the dreamer." I have been fascinated by the intervals with which God tells time.

We often use different watches! In His time, Joseph not only dreamed more dreams and interpreted dreams, he stands out as a type of Christ. His brothers tried to kill his dream—he was falsely accused and imprisoned. But in *God's time,* one morning he woke up in chains, and by afternoon he was second-in-command of a major nation!

Abraham had been promised that he would become the father of many nations, but he had no heir. Sarah was in her nineties when Isaac was born—a child of promise. But a *long*-awaited one!

I can never stop dreaming dreams for God. He has done so much for me. I want everyone to know about who He is, what He has done for them—even those who voted against me! Even those who terrorized my family in Davenport!

Second Samuel carries the story of King David's dreamhouse. His friends had provided a magnificent place for David and his family to live. Then David became aware that there was no place for the ark of the covenant. He determined to build "an exceedingly beautiful" house for God. Inside of it would be a custom-designed place for the ark.

How he dreamed! He drew up plans, and brought in the best craftsmen to put the plans on parchment. The ark was special and treasured because it represented the Holy presence of Jehovah-God. David shared his wonderful vision of a place for God's house with Nathan, the prophet, a special friend and advisor. Nathan must have been like the people on my board. When I have a clear vision they shout, "Go for it, Pastor! Let's do it!"

Suddenly David's vision was dead. He stood back in amazement. He was doing something for God, and the "council" of God voted against it. There would be no temple built by David for God.

I know how David must have felt as the story concluded. Yet he was a man with a right relationship to his disappointments. David had experienced the words of Psalm 37:24, "Though he fall, he shall not be utterly cast down; for the Lord upholdeth him with His hand." David did not stop seeing into the future and dreaming dreams. I am sure he felt disenchanted for a time, but the Bible says he kept on going. He focused on his job as king and, amazingly, right in the difficulty he was able to practice some Selah time! "Then went King David in, and *sat* before the Lord" (2 Sam. 7:18). He took some time to "sit" with the Lord. Something he did with the sheep as a boy. And the refreshment helped him move on, refocus, and be about his Father's business.

It wasn't until Solomon built the temple for the Lord that David's dream was realized. Another interval of God's timing. What excites me is that Solomon gives us some insight into God's expression about our valid dreams when he said,

> Now it was in the heart of David, my father to build an house for the name of the Lord God of Israel. But the Lord said to David my father, Forasmuch as it was in thine heart to build an house for my name, thou didst well in that it was in thine heart. (2 Chron. 6:7-8)

Those verses give me great joy that my lost visions and dreams are not in vain. We rejoice in the victories, but we rejoice too in defeat. God is saying, "Thou didst well in that it was in thine heart." God is not unmindful of our desires toward the Lord. He saw that desire in David and remembered (as God does), and had it recorded through David's son Solomon.

I believe God recorded the welfare mother who gave a large portion of her check to that chapel. He saw each one in my church who was with me in the vision. I believe when the chapel is built—whether I am here or not is not the issue—but because *Jesus never forgets*, He will say, "Tommy Barnett, it was in your heart to build a prayer chapel for Me." That counts for righteousness! Either way, my dream is alive. In reality or in the remembrance of God. Failure and success are both in His care. "For God is not unrighteous to forget your work and labor of love, which ye have shewed toward His name, in that ye have ministered to the saints, and do minister" (Heb. 6:10).

8

The Imperative

IF THERE is one imperative in my life, it is winning souls to Jesus Christ. No matter how many souls I might have won, it is never enough. If I stop bringing people to the Lord or stop bearing fruit, God has the right to cut me off and put someone else behind my pulpit.

One of the threads going through my life is that I must win souls and train people to be soul-winners. I believe that I am a minister to ministers—the people in my congregation. I make no distinctions between the ministers on my staff and the ministers in the pews. All are commanded by God to bring forth fruit. John 15 displays the progression of "fruit bearing" that is required. Fruit! More fruit! Much fruit!

My vision for souls was "caught" from and "taught" by my parents. As a little child I was taught Scripture. One of my early recollections was of my father taking me with him to his revival meetings. He would boost me up on the pulpit and have me quote Scripture to the audience. He also gave me the first word of the verse to get me started.

Being independent and having ideas of my "old nature" even as a primary child, one incident made a lasting impression. This particular church was one where Dad had held revivals before. There were some mischievous boys in that crowd that remembered the preacher brought his little kid to quote verses. They had taken me aside and taught me some mean things in this church. Being half their size I was impressed that they wanted me to be part of their crowd. The results of their input made me feel "big." It made a little guy part of their "in" crowd.

The Scripture Dad had taught me was, "Go ye into all the world and preach the gospel to every creature." The church service commenced. After the songs Dad set me on the pulpit, shared how little Tommy was growing in the Word, and gave me the first word—*go*.

With the word *go* I added the word the boys had dared me to use. Just one word—*home!*

Shocked, my dad encouraged me to say it right. We went through it again: *go*, and I responded, *home!*

As Mother led the song service, Dad quietly took me off the pulpit and down some very creaky stairs to the church basement. He had no trouble locating the boiler room. I knew what that meant. I was familiar with the heat from those situations!

We returned upstairs and went through it again. I longed to be one of the gang. I wanted the approval of those big boys, so to his third try of "go," I shouted, "Home!"

Again my father made his impression, and it was downstairs again, and this time I promised to say it right. To his "go," I raced through ". . . ye into all the world and preach the gospel to every creature."

My grandparents were in attendance that night. They felt it was a mistake for Dad to make me a public example. They told him their feelings. He was undaunted. Mother would plead that I was a "small and nervous child." Dad reminded her he was working on my nervous system!

I often tell a congregation that "the past has no future." However, that part of my past did have a future, for I learned obedience to my father, obedience that was a prerequisite to learning respect and obedience for Father-God. Children must be taught to understand obedience for the sake of obedience. My parents made me practice the piano, accordian, and trombone. I greatly preferred the ballpark to the piano bench, but Dad's desire was getting me ready for the ultimate game of life. I would beg, "If I could just go to the ballpark today, I will practice tonight." His response was predictable. He would start the first word of a Scripture verse: "Now." I knew the words he expected next. "*Now* is the time!" I practiced music, not baseball.

His example made lasting impressions. He preached on street corners, held meetings on courthouse steps, and went from schoolhouse to schoolhouse sharing Christ. He crusaded and broke beer bottles in the street, following the example of his hero, the late, great preacher J. Frank Norris.

I found out that Dad was like the man in the Bible who cared about people, loved children, healed diseases, fed the poor—the man, Jesus. I began to believe that was what everyone was supposed to do. So I followed his example.

I saw evidences of *the* Father in my parents. God expects us in a greater way to feature Him. A. W. Tozer would say, "We are the only God that people will see. Are we evidencing Him on the street corner, in the neighborhood and around the world?" To the challenge of that statement I respond that I, too, want to mirror evidences of my Father. And share His character and salvation with everyone. That is my imperative.

I was sixteen years old when my uncle's church invited my dad to speak for a revival. Dad had responded that it was not possible for him to come, but that his son would be available. Dad said, "Tommy is a chip off the old block!"

The church wrote back, "We don't want the chip, we want the block." He sent me to preach—all one hundred sixteen pounds of me! I started that first evangelistic service thanking the people for coming and telling them, "You folks don't have the 'block,' you have the 'chip'!" God did a wonderful thing that night. At my invitation to accept Jesus, amidst a sandstorm, two young couples came down the aisle. My heart broke from happiness. When I got back to my uncle's, I was so excited I could not sleep. All I thought about was those couples coming to Jesus. (I later learned one couple went to Haiti as missionaries.)

That night, in my spirit, I saw another scene. Multitudes of men and women who would come down the aisle as I preached in years to come. But only if God sent me a sign in Seminole. *That was my first real vision.*

I was to drive my beat-up old car to Seminole, Texas, for the meeting. Much to my surprise as I started out, my mom and dad were following me. They wanted to be sure the car made it there. As I went back to that little church the second night, my mind's eye focused on the faces of those four people who had come to Christ the night before.

If God could give me forty-six more souls, that would be an answer from Him that I was to preach. Fifty souls!

The pastor, my uncle, who had been a twenty-year career missionary in India, was concerned about the "fifty." He told me that my number was a lot for this situation. He explained that Seminole was a tiny town, and he had barely seventy in Sunday school in his church yet. I could not feel discouraged.

As I continued the revival there, the church started to fill up. I was glad Dad had given me a bunch of sermons "just in case I needed them." I did. Sometimes I used the same sermon over again. The music lessons of the past paid off. People loved the accordian, the trombone, and the organ my parents had purchased for me. The music helped bring the crowd.

It was the last night of the revival. I had prayed for fifty. At the close of that final service, four men and two women came down that old aisle. I counted in my almost-unbelieving brain, forty-five . . . forty-six . . . forty-seven . . . forty-eight . . . forty-nine . . . FIFTY!

My uncle and I talked into the night. We were both so excited. Then amidst the celebration I contemplated. Fifty? What if I had asked for one hundred? The Bible says "be it unto you as your faith." There was silence around the kitchen table. Deep inside something was impressing me with the words, Why didn't you ask? Why didn't you ask for more? Across my heart the vision increased, and the sight of people coming grew to a multitude. Within that vision I saw people who were "waiting to be asked."

Some years later I was in a studio in Hollywood, California, recording my first album. Sitting in the background was a man, caught in the shadows, who later introduced himself. He wondered if I had an agent. I told him no. He asked who owned my contract. I said I was free. He pulled up a couple of chairs.

The man had all the trappings of my young perception of Hollywood. The leather notebook, gold pen, and file folder full of contracts. He explained what happens when he "gets a boy a contract." With a silver tongue and a smooth presentation, he had me performing as a star around the world. He tossed around celebrity names. He spoke of Las Vegas and London. It was flattering, even for a young man who was not totally convinced of his degree of talent.

This pending album looked pretty ordinary and homemade in light of his hype. The engineer reminded me we needed to finish the last song. The song was "Poor Man"—one that had been the favorite of the Seminole church. As I sang into the microphone, I saw again the faces of the two young couples who found Christ on that first night in my uncle's church. My heart burst with praise and joy.

I had given the wrong answer to the promoter when he asked if I had a contract. I said, "No, I am free." I realized I did have a contract, and that contract had been placed in the treasury of the Lord. It was signed and irrevocably sealed in the name of the Lord. I was free . . . free to work the works of Him who unmistakenly had called me.

I dropped the expensive, engraved business card onto the table in the reception room. I never saw the man again.

The years went by, and the revivals increased. What inexpressible joy I experienced in winning souls. The imperative grew stronger with every soul. I knew in my heart—for this I was born!

I have always loved the handiwork of God. He has blessed us with such beauty in His creation. It does not surprise me that mountains have been the place where God has been especially close to me. One such time took place when I was nineteen years old. A year was about to end, and the weather was bitingly cold. I was commuting to a television station in St. Joseph, Missouri, each day to make my daily program called "The Singing Parson." In the snow and ice I made the 120-mile roundtrip drive from my parents' home in Kansas City. My throat was beginning to get sore, but I maintained a heavy commitment to prepare and perform. I felt that this was one of God's gracious opportunities to reach many people through television.

My family became concerned and took me to a doctor who, after examining me, said I should have total rest for several months. The doctor said that without a rest from preaching and singing, I could lose my voice and permanently injure my vocal chords.

We went to New Mexico, where the air was hot and dry. I basked in the sun. During this time another "Son" shone on me through the Holy Spirit with a clear message that my spiritual health could also be improved. God was saying to me that I needed a closer walk with Him. I desired to learn the meaning of "waiting on the Lord."

One of those days in New Mexico, Mother, Dad, and I drove south across the border into Mexico. As we came into Monterrey, on the distant horizon were tall, magnificent mountains. We kept traveling toward those mountains. At the foot of their beauty, we found a local hotel, situated on the edge of a plateau. The next morning, I mounted a donkey to take the long trek up toward the top of those peaks. It was a challenge with the rugged trails and tight corners. A sure-footed donkey carried me up, up to the summit. The beauty was breathtaking. Almost at the summit we stopped at a place called Horsetail Falls. As the donkey grazed, I sat beside a pool of still water. My spirit soared. I praised God for all He was and for the carpet of beauty He had rolled out that day—just for His junior evangelist. I left the mountain with new strength. My voice was strong. I could not wait to get down to the valley below which represented "fields white unto harvest" and new opportunities to win souls.

The Philadelphia Opera House was jammed. I was to preach. It was an awesome experience. This great house presented me with a unique scene that contained a "flashback" and a "flash-forward." The flashback was to when I was young, and my dad had taken me to hear the legendary Charles E. Fuller. Each Sunday with his Old-Fashioned Revival Hour program and quartet, he packed the Long Beach Municipal Auditorium. Scores of souls were consistently saved. As I sat there watching, I felt in my heart I would be used in similar places to win souls. The flash-forward was an image of a church that would seat seven thousand and have three balconies—just like the Philadelphia Opera House. It was a picture of our present facility today!

I became aware that the same God who was with me in Seminole, Texas, was present. The same vision of seeing multitudes who needed to be "asked" if they wanted to receive Jesus Christ as Savior was evident.

My travels took me overseas. Again, multitudes in the valley of decision. I traveled forty thousand miles and preached the same gospel. I went through Communist-bloc countries; preached in Paris, France; traveled through Switzerland; and stood in Berlin—a divided city. Souls on both sides of that then barricaded wall needed Jesus.

I walked the Via Dolorosa, stood close to the top of Golgotha. I saw India with its poverty and faceless hordes of people, but all known to God. How would it be possible to ever tell them all about the love and sufficiency of God? My heart was heavy with compassion when the tens of thousands of lost souls filled soccer stadiums, open fields, and jammed town squares.

On these trips the consciousness that *people count, so we count people* was coming into focus—a saying ready to be called up when I started in my own church.

The missionaries met me in China and Hong Kong. What trophies the missionaries are to God! Again the masses of humanity burdened my heart.

In Japan, a country known for its respect for the elderly, I felt younger than my years. I had no signs of age or wisdom. God must pour His maturity into me to be respected by the people. In our first meeting I had been warned that in Japan you do not give an altar call. Altar calls had never been optional in the Barnett experience. I prayed for wisdom. At the close, I broke the rule. With the grace and poise for which the Japanese are known, a young person came to the front. More followed. God confirmed His call is without repentance . . . altar calls included.

In the Philippines, the Manila school kids called me "G.I. Joe!" The young people were wonderful. We had fun singing and having a big time with them. I sang to the accompaniment of the missionaries' instruments. It continued into the night. Kids mobbed me, rubbing my arms (Americans have hair, their arms did not!). The song service finally had to stop so I could preach. I promised *one* more song. Much to the kids' delight, I announced the last one as a favorite of Elvis Presley. They roared. We were in the square of Manila, and by the time I had finished "Peace in the Valley," the crowd had grown to ten thousand.

I had a Filipino interpreter. He was so excited. He was like an alter ego. When I raised an arm, he copied. When I clenched my fist, so did he. When I got real soft, he diminuendoed. What a team we were!

At the close I said to the throng they could leave that Manila square and know for sure they would live with Jesus in eternity. Someone said the hands went up "like a forest of brown palms" as I gave an altar call. A leading disc jockey was one of those hands that reached up for eternal life. He began playing "His Hand in Mine" on his radio show. That was the beginning of a Christian song becoming top on the foreign and American charts!

Jesus said, "The field is the world!" I was beginning to know what he meant by that declaration. My focus now was like a window on the world. A world without God and without hope. I could never do the task alone. I needed to start pouring this vision into people.

The last words the Lord spoke on earth were the words Dad taught me: "Go ye into all the world and preach the gospel to every creature." A man's last words must be significant. Their significance is written all over the New Testament. Heaven and hell are both real places.

A CHURCH WHERE EVERYONE COULD COME AND GET SAVED

My dream of a church "where everyone could come and get saved" became a reality. After the long miles of travel, I interned as an assistant pastor with my father for two years. However, it did not fill the desire of my heart. Advisers and others felt I was foolish to leave such a strong ministry as an evangelist—especially to become a servant, for in my heart that was the definition of my concept of a pastor. A call from Davenport, Iowa, presented the challenge to go and do what was active in my heart. I had already surveyed other churches, looked into the lives of great men, and now had my parameters for a church in place.

In a church that kept pastors scarcely two years, I began my program to reach the lost. The response came quickly. First through a dedicated lady in the church who also loved souls, and then the contagious challenge for the church to become soul-winners. Before long three thousand had made decisions for Christ in just one year. A soul-winning church had emerged. Now these must be trained, for growth was inevitable. My philosophy—*a church that does not grow is sick*—remains to this day. I am intent on the New Testament church model that was added to "daily."

The program I brought to Westside Assembly was centered in soul-winning. Many churches have too many activities. My new church was not an exception. I did not seek to kill the previous church activities, I just let some die a natural death. They were replaced with my first imperative—soul-winning.

Training soul-winners was part of the vision to help reach the world. Careful attention to needs and people is part of this training. At Westside, I produced a five-fold program for winning the lost.

- Show the person his or her lost condition
- Point out the consequences of lostness
- Show how the lost came to Jesus

- Explain that Jesus saves
- Show the person how to be saved

At Phoenix, the program expanded, but the basics remain. My heartbeat for souls comes from God. I am convinced the whole world can be reached if people are willing to accept God's plan of evangelism.

The first pyramid program was God's. It is one-to-one sharing. If everyone did that, we would gain the world, and there would be no lost souls.

Telling people to win the lost to Christ is nothing like showing them. I strive to do that repeatedly. People see it, witness the results, and are motivated to obey the command of God. He sets the example; therefore, soul-winning becomes a way of life.

Historically, during World War II, Korea, and Vietnam, people became familiar with the giant posters colored in rich red, white, and blue, with a portrait of a man with his arm outstretched. The caption was powerful: "Uncle Sam needs YOU!"

Phoenix First Assembly members display a similar banner proudly across their hearts. Their message—"God needs YOU!" And people are recruited into God's army.

Newcomers and new believers are encouraged to join the Saturday Soul-Winning Society. It is a compact, clear program on how to lead others to the Lord. Under strong leadership they study the concepts of the book of Romans. Next they receive "hands-on" training as witnesses. One set of statistics relayed that after a ten-week period more than a hundred teams, combining a "prospective soul-winner" with a "seasoned soul-winner," accounted for an excess of fifteen hundred decisions for Christ. An observer noted that was enough people to start another large church!

Does the "fruit" remain? The stories are legion of men, women, and children coming to faith through the Saturday Soul-Winning Society.

Al and Peggy Alexander, who are responsible for preparing and conducting a meeting each Saturday of the year, tell the story of a young man named Scott Olsen.

Scott was in their group and eager to share his faith. He had learned the principles, and was appropriating the next phase of the society called discipleship. He met Richard Dong and led him in the sinner's prayer. He not only led Richard to Christ, but he started teaching him over the next year. Scott invited Richard to move in with him so they could have more quality time. He helped him grow spiritually and assisted him in finding a job. When Richard was on his economic and spiritual feet, he moved into his own place.

Richard met another unsaved man and led him to Christ. He discipled him just as Scott had nurtured him. Now Richard is attending Bible school. What is Richard's potential for more souls? Great! It continues to grow, just as Scott's before him and his new child of God with him. They are all rejoicing in Psalm 2:8, "Ask of me, and I shall give thee the heathen for thine inheritance, and the uttermost parts of the earth for thy possession."

My *imperative* remains unchanged . . . with increasing thousands of others who have chosen that same "imperative" as their own. *Daily*, people are being added to the church.

PART THREE

Pro-Vision

9

What's in
Your House?

THERE IS a miracle in every house! Everything you need to build a great church may be found within your house! What a revelation. How liberating! Pastors look everywhere but within their own house to find the resources and people needed to do great exploits for God.

From the time I started growing churches, I learned a valuable lesson. Look "within," for sitting in one of your pews is the person needed to fill your need. I know. My staff has almost entirely come from within the house. And the miracles we see daily are results of our people being willing to search their own hearts to find what God can use.

I believe God wants to get every church ready for awesome things if we are not allergic to the preparation. It takes work. It takes prayer. It takes commitment. I challenge you to pronounce open season on what is within your house. You will find the implications of this truth astounding and life changing. The key that unlocks the door to New Testament growth!

It is biblical to ask the question, What is in your house? Elisha, the man of God, asked the question centuries ago. And the story centers on God's pro-vision.

GOD WILL SUPPLY—WE MUST APPLY

This Bible vignette revolves around a widow with two sons. She had needs to be met and hurts to be healed. She was not unlike other women in the inner cities of America today. She was penniless, had no husband, and no visible means of support. Her landlord was about to evict her. Compounding the drama was the fact that the land was in famine. Even with money, there was little available food. In every way, this woman fit the profile and had the potential of becoming "the original bag lady."

The recorded story from 2 Kings 4:1-7 reads as follows:

> Now there cried a certain woman of the wives of the sons of the prophets unto Elisha, saying, Thy servant my husband is dead; and thou knowest that thy servant did fear the Lord: and the creditor is come to take unto him my two sons to be bondsmen. And Elisha said unto her, What shall I do for thee? Tell me, *what hast thou in the house?* And she said, Thine handmaid hath *not any thing* in the house *save a pot of oil.*
>
> Then he said, Go, borrow thee vessels abroad of all thy neighbours, even empty vessels; borrow not a few. And when thou art come in, thou shalt shut the door upon thee and upon thy sons, and shalt pour out into all those vessels, and thou shalt set aside that which is full.
>
> So she went from him, and shut the door upon her and upon her sons, who brought the vessels to her; and *she poured* out.
>
> And it came to pass, when the vessels were full, that she said unto her son, Bring me yet a vessel. And he said unto her, There is not a vessel more. And the oil stayed.
>
> Then she came and told the man of God. And he said, Go, sell the oil, and pay thy debt, and live thou and thy children on the rest. (emphasis added)

She was in the midst of a dilemma. Fortunately, she knew where to turn—to the man of God. In today's anxiety society, would to God that more of the poor, needy, and afflicted knew where to turn. If only we could get the message across that the New Testament church has doors wide open to needs. The people of God are available to minister to those needs, for every member is a minister.

Elisha's resume offered tremendous ministry accomplishments. In the past he had been the part of a miracle which supplied the needs of a whole army. He was instrumental in subduing a takeover attempt by the rebellious people of Moab. Yet he was touched by the hurting of a poor widow. He had time to listen, and counsel and minister to her. When her husband lived, she and her sons were nourished. When he died, they became disposable people—except to God.

In inquiring of her need, the man of God asked a natural question, *What is in your house?* She was slow to respond. She knew it was empty. Every drawer and cooler and cupboard was stripped. She said, "Nothing except a jar of oil."

How easy it is to say "nothing." And then remember a trinket or a trivial jar of oil. Like when Jesus fed the multitude. Nothing except two fish and five loaves from a child that Andrew, his disciple, had discovered. A child willing to share his catch with Jesus. What was so little was the needed thing. What was so small was the key thing.

EVERYTHING GREAT STARTS WITH SMALL THINGS

Elisha challenged the widow: "Go" (a verb of action). He did not say, "Pray about it, or consider this, or let me contemplate for a time." Instead, "Go thou and borrow vessels from your neighbors and don't get just a few." It is fascinating that this is advice to a woman who already was heavily in debt. Now she is being told to "go and borrow again."

There has to be a spiritual principle. We are to "borrow when borrowing will bring a good return." When borrowing provides a positive expectation because God will work through our expectations if they are toward Him.

When Peter and John went to the temple, at the hour of prayer, they noticed a man sitting at the gate who had not walked for almost forty years. Peter said, "Look on us." He did, and as he looked he expected to receive something from them. Possibly silver or gold or at least a coin. Peter provided this man a new experience. He related, "Silver and gold have I none, but Go [an action word] and you will walk." The lame man's expectation was money. When the man of God is involved, watch out for the results—results that may be contrary to natural expectations. These were. He walked!

We are clearly reminded by a God who desires to receive all who come to Him, that we all are agents to bring that relief and hope—even to an insolvent widow. As Christ's workers we need to enlarge our own expectations of what He wants to do in our lives and the lives of those to whom we minister.

While stretching expectations, it is realized that God provides more than adequate *pro-vision* by "taking our nothingness and linking it to His Almightiness." That is the touchpoint where things begin to happen. The eternal life of God is in us. His life is interfaced with ours. The stunning truth of Romans 5:17 is potent: "For if by the transgression of the one, death reigned, through the one, much more those who receive the abundance of grace and of the gift of righteousness will *reign in life* through the One, Jesus Christ" (emphasis added).

Christ by His death on Calvary took our sin. What happened to His life? It came to us, His children. "Christ in you the hope of glory!" "Because I live, you too will live!" "I am come that you might have life, and have it *more* abundantly." Therefore we "reign in life through the One, Jesus Christ." And we reign in righteousness and pro-vision. We "live and move and breathe in Him." Constantly He wants to stretch us, even as Elisha was stretching the faith of the destitute widow.

How we need our faith to be stretched. Spurgeon described faith as an Action, based upon a Belief, supported by the Confidence that God does what He says,

Forever oh Lord, Thy word is settled in heaven. (Ps. 119:89)

God is not a man that He should lie nor the Son of man that he should repent. Hath He said and shall He not do it? Hath He spoken and shall He not make it good? (Num. 23:19)

That "forever-settled word" and the integrity of God are the foundational basis of the ABC's of faith that allow us to get ready for miracles.

Action—Belief—Confidence

These are predecessors to miracles in every house. The widow was to borrow, and not just a few containers. When this was accomplished, she was to "go in" and shut the door behind her. Why "go in" and "shut the door?" Our Lord said that "Thy Father which seeth in secret Himself shall reward thee openly" (Matt. 6:4).

There are times when great ideas and visions come into our heads. We race to tell our friends and associates. We hurry home to tell our family how we are on tiptoes to see what God can accomplish. So many times, this is where the vision dies. Those around us see the negatives, not the positives. Those "why" phrases come into play. Why you don't have time! You don't have the resources! Why would you want to do that? Let others take risks. A thousand reasons "why" have a way of retarding action and crushing a dream. At a time like this, we must look for the *portrait of pro-vision*. Seal it within our hearts and move with God on the potentiality.

Surely this widow did not need a fresh vision of her need. She lived with it. Her perception was more than likely that, in going to the man of God and reminding him her husband had been a pious man, a minister, "a son of the prophets," she would evoke sympathy. Her mate had died with a stack of bills left behind. Those feared "repossessing teams" of creditors were intimidating her with the threat that they would take her sons as slaves. To the poverty would be the added loss of her children. It appeared there were no options, until she went to the man of God and experienced a *re-vision*. Deep within her desperation she hoped for charity. Maybe a portion of the "poor box," common in that time, could be shared with her family. Instead, she was about to experience pro-vision that would *exceed* her need!

There had to be great exhilaration and wonderment as she listened to and acted on the suggestion of the man of God. "Go . . . shut the door."

If she had run next door and explained the reasons they were borrowing jars and vessels, her expectation would have been killed. Can't you hear the gossip? "Why empty vessels when they are hungry? Why would she want the jars that are stacked on the back porch with nothing inside? Shouldn't she ask for something of substance?"

Going "in" and "shutting the door" allows you to shut out those who say nothing is going to happen. Literally it is an opportunity to shut the door on the negatives. While in that quiet place, *"Remember not the former things. I will do a new thing."* Inside the quiet place the distractions are removed. The doubting Thomases are disallowed. The extraneous is stripped away. God-sized tasks are performed. At that sacred place the pro-vision of God is placed in that incubator of the heart. And the response is again that *God can do everything . . . but fail!*

Literally, the Bible says the widow and her sons went inside, with the pots and jars and vessels stacked—as high as their expectations—and began to pour! Faith was the substance of the pouring, an evidence of *action, belief,* and *confidence* at work. When she tipped her meager last jar of oil to fill another vessel, the miracle started. The pouring signified "God and I are in this together." She became linked up in the enterprises of Holy God whose storehouses are full of pro-vision. The miracle was already in her house.

That same question, What is in your house? has a wealth of application in our personal lives. It continues to compound as the question is addressed to the church, What is in your house and the house of God? The answers run rampant—nothing . . . nothing. On occasion, a nothing *except!* Somehow people focus on how little they have and how little they can give. People are unaware that a miracle is in every house, including God's house. Never miss the potential of the little you have. It may be small according to your need, but *little is much when God is in it.*

Avalanches develop from a tiny snowflake. That baby in the manger grew to become the Lord of hosts, which *is* King of kings and Lord of lords!

I remember overviewing my church in Davenport right after I had been called as pastor. It didn't appear to me there was much in that house. It seated less than one hundred people. The stairs were cracked, the paint had peeled, and windows were broken. I preached with no visible results for three weeks. That had been unheard of in my past evangelistic ministry.

Yet *within that house* was a woman who had quietly been visiting in her neighborhood week after week, with no visible results. She wanted to bring people to Jesus. We got together with one of her friends and started visiting. The first week there were no results. But the next week, when I went to pick up the women, one was waving frantically at me. She had an old man on his knees wanting to get saved. She didn't know what to do!

I led him to Christ, and the next Sunday he was in the front row testifying. People got excited. Each week we brought the new converts for the members to see. The soul-winners increased to six. All from within the house!

That first woman was filling her car and her husband's each week. Then they started making two trips. When we asked the church for a bus, it was that same woman, who through the sale of a house, came up with a thousand dollars to purchase our first bus. The people, the finances, the desire—all were found in the house of God among just seventy-six people. Naturally and supernaturally we grew! *There was a miracle within the house!*

In Phoenix we had a deacon who sat on our board. He was a faithful member, but his business went into reversals. Because of a failing business, he felt he should resign. I would not hear of it. Gary Allison came on board with his skills and expertise and became our business manager.

I have always looked for character above skill in men. I knew he had the first, and believed God for the skill. Little did we know at that time that this man, whom I would not allow to quit, was God's man for the position.

As we started building buildings and expanding, his expertise was astonishing. Our business transactions have become a model for scores of churches. Sitting right on our deacon board was the man for all seasons of our development. Again, there was a miracle within the house. I firmly believe that great churches are built from within. After beginning it may have appeared that some of these people had "nothing except" and the "except" proved to be exceptional!

LITTLE SIGNS HAVE GREAT SIGNIFICANCE

Elijah, another prophet of God, lived in a time of famine. There had been no rain or precipitation for three and one-half years. He was an *unknown* in his time. The Bible records nothing of his parentage, and the place he was to have come from, Thisbe, is an unfamiliar place set in a mountainous region.

He is a solid example to those who protest, "I can't do anything for God because I have no credentials. I didn't come from roots of opportunity." Neither did Elijah, to our knowledge. He was called from comparative obscurity. Yet one day he made an incredible announcement. "There will be no rain until I announce it!" Was this an arrogant statement from an unknown man? It appears no angel came to give him a revelation. He found his way into the king's palace and shared his declaration: "As the Lord God of Israel liveth, before whom I stand, there shall not be dew nor rain these years, but according to *my* word" (1 Kings 17:1, emphasis added).

After years of drought, the Lord told him to revisit the palace, and carry the information that God would send rain on the earth. What gave confidence to Elijah? Being sensitive to God and God's Word. Years before in Deuteronomy Elijah had noted, "If you worship idols in this land that I have given you for a promise I will shut up the heavens and not let it rain anymore." God's Word had taken residence in Elijah's heart. He acted according to the Word, an *action*, based on the Deuteronomy statement, supported by the unswerving *belief* of who God was, and the *confidence* that God and His Word are one.

The story is familiar. In the sky, Elijah saw a cloud that was just about the size of a man's fist. A small thing. A nonspectacular symbol. And when he saw it, he had his servants ready the chariot to inform King Ahab it was starting to rain!

Only a cloud. Just two fish and five loaves. A small jar of oil! Nothing except! God then shows Himself willing and able to perform. "Be it unto you, even as your faith." "Now unto Him that is able to do exceedingly abundantly above all that we can ask or think, according to the power that worketh in us" (Eph. 3:20).

Congregations must address the question, What is in your house? Is there faith? Surely even mustard-seed faith is present. Faith that God can take what is insignificant and multiply it according to God's unlimited multiplication ability.

Sitting in the congregation one Sunday was a man of retirement age. For most of his life he had been a lay minister. During this senior season of life he had been involved with the growing Deaf Ministry at Phoenix First Assembly. He was faithful and caring in performing the work of the Lord. In the past he had been effective in hospital visitation. In reference to "what is in your house?" a seed was planted. He recognized the church was exploding. That the pressures were making hospital visitation a major area of need within church life to be addressed.

Sitting across the desk from me, in great mutuality, Alvin Booher shared his vision of reaching people in hospitals. "Pastor, I'll be glad to represent you when I go to the hospitals." It was agreed, and he became my arm extended, throughout Phoenix. In 1988 he made approximately seven thousand hospital calls. More than fifteen hundred prayed to receive Jesus Christ and were followed up. He has redefined hospital visitation. In the beginning, his "jar of annointing oil" was only a few ounces. Today, it should be purchased in case lots. Every year is a rewarding year for this man who gives all the glory to God for what He has done.

His countenance shines as he recounts the miracles that God has performed in the lives of the sick, infirm, the deaf, and even among the hospital staff. No one will convince him that it is not possible, for "The prayer of faith to save the sick, and the Lord shall raise him up; and if he has committed sins, they shall be forgiven him."

To many who have recovered, this church has become their place of worship. Their ever-flowing testimonies to the power of God in their lives and the love of Pastor Booher is a challenge to those a fraction of his age. Many hospitals in the Phoenix area call him their chaplain. He keeps a careful record—visitations, salvations, rededications, communions, annointings with oil, those with whom he prays, those who choose to have no prayer, the funerals he conducts—all are recorded in stenographic detail.

He loves being "that arm extended," and thanks God for the times he has been touched in body through the prayers of the church. He lives in the Psalm 84 promise of "They go from strength to strength." This miracle-working man came from *within the house!*

Some years ago one of the men he had visited wanted to provide him with better transportation. Much to his surprise, he donated a new Chevrolet El Camino truck. It was presented to Alvin Booher in a "This Is Your Life" setting at the church. The El Camino was driven right onto the platform as a symbol of love from a patient who was blessed by this man.

It was accepted with a sense of "unworthiness" from a humble and gentle man who found in the *house* of his heart, room for thousands of needy people.

It is often recommended that our people put a searchlight into their *inner house* to be sure the Holy Spirit is there and at work. *When the Holy Spirit is at work in the inner house, things are accomplished from the inside out.*

What trips the multiplication process?

For the widow with her oil, it was when, by faith, *she started pouring!* The principle is the same today. With what you have, you begin to *pour.* Your talent increases as God pours His love on you.

What is in your house? You may be surprised. Women know when they need extra cash that a garage sale brings results. Successful businessmen attest, "The harder I work, the luckier I get." Children needing funds collect cans and pop bottles, newspapers, and do errands. There is usually a way to fill a need!

A family down on their luck discovered a lottery ticket in their house. They checked its worth, and found they had a treasure. A couple with seven children, from a low socioeconomic background, looked inside their house and recognized those seven children were gold. They began "pouring" into the children: love, caring, education, and godly principles. They gave away their poorly tuned television and let the children develop their own programming—with handmade puppets and stories written on the backs of envelopes, pondered under a big oak tree. They have discovered free museums, parks with recreational opportunities, and church affairs that nourish and enrich their future.

Within seven months the dramatic change in that home was visible. Teachers lauded the children's progress in school. Sunday school teachers were amazed at the help even the little ones were in acting out Bible stories and wanting to participate.

"Every wise woman buildeth her house" (Prov. 14:1). This mother, with the help and concern of her husband, is doing just that. They are becoming architects of their family, using the only Guidebook that is the basis of a family being "rooted and built up in Him and established in the faith, as you have been taught" (Col. 2:7). What a resource of inestimable value is *within the house* of all parents who have been entrusted with children.

What's in your house is a question to consider when there is discouragement or depression. Where hate resides and understanding is at a premium, unforgiving feelings are swept under the carpets of grudges and phobias. God calls His people to clean house. Every individual is faced with choices when it comes to letting the bitter make one better or worse. That was what Calvary was all about. What is in your house has to do with the way you think, act, and react: *"As a man thinketh in his heart, so is he."*

Take your thoughts to the Lord. Go into a quiet place alone, and together with God make plans for what you will use that is already in your house. In that quiet place God was aware I had been pressed and encouraged to write a book. I had rejected many well-meaning manuscripts. Then, from within the house came Michael Clifford, one of my

EPIC team. Michael's life had been devasting outside of Christ. In Christ his indomitable spirit and unselfish work provided the means to an invitation of Thomas Nelson, Inc., to publish this book—not from the scores of publishers, but from within this house!

Rarely be impressed with other people's thoughts on what you should do. Look for firsthand revelation. God speaks to us through His Word into our brain. We all can develop the mind of Christ. Our transformations and empowerments come from above and move into our house. "If God is for you, who can be against you." And remember, "no weapon formed against you will prosper" when your house is sealed with Christ in God.

This message on "What is in your house?" has spread like a house afire. The response has been heartening. Lots of priorities are being rearranged as the house, which is the temple of the Holy Spirit, is going through some dramatic refurbishing and some de-accumulating.

One evening I was sharing the story of our "church with a heart" on national television. Sitting on a couch with his dad in Greenville, Texas, was Keith Buchanan, a butcher by trade. He was impressed on hearing our philosophy of meeting needs and healing hurts. The next day he borrowed some money and bought a ticket to come to Phoenix and see what was happening. The next Sunday morning he sat on the front row, smiling. After the service he introduced himself and began a conversation with a question: "Do you know there are four hundred thousand-plus senior citizens in the Valley of the Sun?" He tacked on a statement that really caught my attention. "How is your church reaching those people?" The next sentence was a request for a job. "If you hire me, I'll help you reach them!"

As a pastor, I knew nothing of Keith Buchanan, but was aware of the vision he had "caught" and which was reflected in his eyes. In his "house" was a willingness to fill a need among immobile seniors.

Keith was told there were no funds at the present for the project. He was not deterred. He moved his family to Phoenix and began as a volunteer. His first order of business was locating the seniors—learning who lived in nursing homes or who were confined in their own homes. People who in the past had been faithful to the church: the former prayer warriors, the faithful tithers, the ladies aid, the missionaries. Initially, there were about thirty in our area.

Keith obtained thirty cassette players and took them to these shut-ins. He saw to it they heard my sermons each week. Soon he had a bus, and began picking them up and bringing those who could be transported to the "house" of the Lord.

Pastors should not forget these people were once in their prime. As Keith Buchanan had realized, when these dear ones were young they were able to give. The pastors needed them. They were of value. When they were healthy, they helped build, cooked meals, taught Sunday school. Some of the women had been former "casserole queens" of church suppers—others, faithful choir members or deacons. Some had never missed Wednesday night and had been on the missionaries' support team, and more than once they had "prayed down the power" when there were needs. Now they were in need and had been left on a shelf—out of sight and often out of mind. To Keith, the former butcher, now on staff, these people in his terms were "U.S. Choice, Prime, and a cut above." His love for them spread until he had thirty teams of workers going into the convalescent centers.

The ministry grew, and older members or those who had become prematurely ill were brought back into God's house by love, and were a functioning part of the body they had been instrumental in building. Some time passed. One day Keith came again for a discussion, this time as a valued assistant. He saw the need of program support. He was aware that I was doing everything from preaching to pounding nails on props for the big events the church produces. Keith watched me spend hours working with productions, putting up and tearing down sets. He believed he could help. It sounded good. I let him loose! The ultimate outcome was Creative Media Productions.

His goal and primary objective is not building a bigger prop or a more spectacular living flag. The distinctive purpose is "that souls might be saved from eternal hell." Keith loves to say, "Thank God for ever-changing methods to reach the world with the never-changing gospel." He agrees with the apostle Paul, who wrote, "I am made all things to all men, that I might save some" (1 Cor. 9:22).

When asked in Pastors' School where talent can be found to help reach goals, pastors must be encouraged to look and see *what is already in the house*. Maybe turning a corner, and across the street, will be a butcher shop where another Keith Buchanan is looking to find needs and fill them.

Christians long to do something for God. It is innate. Look in your church and see if you can't find an abundance of workers already resident in God's house. Never overlook the youngsters. When I was about nine years old, I felt the stirring in my heart to God's work. From childhood, I was taught what service was all about. And I was blessed with seeing results and watching my parents live in "open house" for God and man.

A little boy from the projects was spellbound with an illustrated sermon. He had been riding our bus for about two months. He lived with his aunt and a lot of cousins, kittens, and other kids. He had been told the story of "Whosoever's House" by a Sunday school teacher. She had carefully gone through the details of John 3:16 with the emphasis on "*Whosoever* believeth in Him should not perish but have everlasting life."

He had heard over and over about the many things that went into "Whosoever's house." Selfishness. Stealing. Squealing. Cheating. Lying. He also was impressed that Jesus wanted to be "his friend," and that God wanted to replace these things in his house with unselfishness, honesty, truth, and trust.

This little guy had many forces pulling against him that made it difficult for him to comprehend these truths. He just liked the thought of life being likened to a house, and the name Whosoever was the funniest name he had ever heard. In fact, he called his skinny cat Whoso just for kicks!

One Sunday his busload got to see a special illustrated sermon. It was called "Fatal Attractions." The setting was familiar to the kid. Crack, cocaine, theft—things that were everyday events in his block. For the first time he saw Satan portrayed as a "real guy" tempting him and his friends. He saw the blockades he had to overcome if he could ever find his way to heaven. Success, fame, the promise of fortune were all portrayed as blockades.

Satan, the accuser, spoke like he was speaking directly to the bus kid:

No one really cares about you.
There are too many phony people.
Who does God think He is anyway?
Go ahead and do your own thing.
This church is just taking you for a ride.

But the bus kid kept thinking about the *wrong things* and the right things that should go into Whosoever's house. When the illustrated sermon was over, he ran with a lot of other bus kids to the front. He didn't want a part of those fatal attractions. He wanted to be sure that "Whosoever believeth in Him should not perish but have everlasting life." He needed the assurance that Whosoever meant *him*.

A few weeks later the kid told his friend, "Someday I'm gonna' give one of those 'sock-it-to-'em kinda' illustrated sermons. Someday I'm doin' something BIG for God."

Someday that kid will be pouring!

Is it worth the time and trouble to produce and present these events? Is it worth it to carry the insurance up to two hundred thousands dollars per year to keep the buses relicensed? The answer? What is the worth of a soul? A lost soul, picked up from the ghetto, put on a bus, placed in a Sunday school class, picnicked on special occasions, loved and loved some more? The worth is inestimable. The price was God's Son, so all the Whosoevers can have everlasting life.

Volunteers at Phoenix First Assembly experience days of weariness in the work of God. It is natural. Yet it is difficult to find one truly discouraged. They are convinced the best antidote for discouragement is to win a soul to Jesus Christ. Problems decrease when people win souls, fill needs, and heal hurts.

What's in your house? A legion of workers will tell you their inner house is full of thanks and praise for the opportunity to serve the Lord with gladness in whatever capacity they have been called. Although most will admit that finding a need and filling it is not glamorous business. It might have its peaks at Pastors' Conferences or when individuals are called to go to other churches to share their proven skills. Most work harder in the church than they do in their employment.

Thanks may be offered or forgotten. It is not an issue. They know who they are ministering to—the Lord Himself. For "if you work with the least of these you minister to Me." Most attest to the fact that you need to be needed more than you need to be appreciated. When you decide to start filling needs, then you must decide to do it for the joy of winning souls and healing hurts, rather than for the gratitude received. The cross is the focus, on this side of eternity. On the other side, the crowns await. God is never unmindful of obedience and faithfulness.

Many workers have left their positions and ministers quit the ministry because of not being appreciated. That is wrong. To be appreciated is the worst reason in the world for reaching out in compassion to anybody. Rather, we are privileged to be co-laborers with Christ. Herein lies the secret of the inhouse loving and powerful staff and volunteers at Phoenix First Assembly. They have their spiritual priorities in line. They are ministering to Christ. They have learned what it means to keep pouring the oil of their love and Christ's care into people. And the more they pour, the more they are filled with the endless supply of God.

Also to be recognized are those that are blessed with this world's goods who have chosen to take much financially from their house of resource and pour into the lives of those less fortunate and needy through their financial means. Everyone is aware that no matter what the cultural or financial standing, the ground is very level at the foot of the cross. All are taught to consider seriously "What is in *your* house?" And then look for the miracle. The touching story of Elisha and the poor widow motivates this church. "Go and do likewise."

If this 2 Kings experience were set in the twentieth-century mode, it could read as follows, as a tribute to those who have become "house miracles" for the glory of God:

Now there were a multitude of helpless, poor, homeless, and discarded people. Some were old and feeble, some were but children. All were familiar with the bill collectors, drug dealers, and gangs of the day. The pawn shops and liquor stores lined the streets. Drugs, sin, and addiction were the norm of the day and the threat of the violent nights.

Behold, one day, the forgotten became aware that the people of God were in the city. Some inquired of the people of God if they would provide some bread and raiment and shelter. Their pleas had fallen on uninterested ears in the past. They felt discarded like trash in an alley.

The people of God asked, "What is in your house?" Most replied, "I have no house." With perception, the people of God saw human resources within these tragedies. They had a vision of men, women, and children to be reclaimed and restored.

The people of God said to the street people, "Come, bring with you all the empty-vesseled people you can locate and not a few. We know of a storehouse that has riches that are not counted in money, and joy that is not measured in circumstances.

The people pondered among themselves. Some shut their cardboard doors and within paper-thin walls discussed this invitation to come. An invitation unlike any heard on the streets before.

With faltering faith and hitherto tarnished hope they came as empty vessels. Men, women, and especially the children. They were brought to God's house.

And the people of God started *pouring* themselves and their God into the hearts and lives of the people on the street. And the *pouring* has never ceased.

The results were visible: "The people which sat in darkness saw a great light; and to them which sat in the region and shadow of death light is sprung up" (Matt. 4:16).

The rewards are eternal. God's people taking what is in their houses and depositing those "gifts of God" into the treasury of the Lord!

What is in your house? Let me assure you there *is* a miracle in your house!

10

The Treasury of the Lord

THE UNITED STATES Department of the Treasury offers a sort of mystique. This department is responsible for the management of the national finances. It issues government bonds and treasury certificates; oversees the collection of customs and the IRS. Part of the fascination of the United States treasury is that it coins metallic money and engraves and prints our paper currency.

For some reason, a certain mystique also surrounds the treasury of the Lord. Charles Hadden Spurgeon, from his Park Street pulpit, preached on the subject. He saw himself as "a minister sent to announce with terrible earnestness the truth of God." Although his writings and sermons were eloquent, he expounded hard truth: "What was God's was God's and what God said, He meant." I have been fascinated by the important implications of these treasury truths in the lives of Christians. It is a heavy subject and one that merits our attention and study.

There was obviously an urgency in the mind of the apostle Paul when he said, "I beseech you therefore, brethren, by the mercies of God, that you present your bodies a living sacrifice, *holy, acceptable* to God, which is your reasonable service" (Rom. 12:1, emphasis added).

There are two words in that "beseeching" that I would like to underscore—two words that are the focus of this chapter. They are *holy* and *acceptable*. God's people need to assimilate this teaching. It will literally be transforming. The word *holy* in the Bible is translated *sanctified*. The word does not mean sinless perfection. It does not mean perfect. Sanctified means set aside or dedicated for a particular purpose.

When I stand in my pulpit at our church, I am standing in front of a sanctified pulpit, because it is set aside for preaching of God's Word. I have jerked on it; I have tried to put my fist through it; I have torn the hinges off of it as passionate men of God tend to do. My pulpit has a lot of emphasis markings! In no way is it a perfect pulpit, but it is a sanctified pulpit.

I own a black suit that I use only when I am preaching the gospel of Jesus Christ. The suit lining is torn out in a few places. If I am not careful, I stick my hand in the wrong hole and go down to the lining. It is not a perfect suit of clothes, but it is a sanctified suit. I do not go golfing in that suit. I do not go to my boys' sports events in that suit. This is a sanctified suit because it is set apart.

At times when I look at that suit, I smile inside with an accompanying tear in my heart, remembering my dad's old black suit—the suit I found in his closet when I went to preach his funeral service. My sanctified suit went to his funeral. Dad's hung in the closet, shiny and worn, a symbol of thousands of services—a sanctified suit that dressed my father for the work of God. (Now he is clothed in heaven's attire, where the shine is a reflection of that eternal city.)

Sanctification or being holy is never to be confused with perfection. It is by simple definition *being set apart for service unto God*. When something became sanctified for God in the Bible, people were not to touch it. It was literally set apart for God. This example was clear in the Old Testament. There was a small piece of furniture called the ark of the covenant in the Holy of Holies in the tabernacle.

And they shall construct an ark . . . and you shall overlay it with pure gold, . . . and you shall put into the ark the testimony which I will give you . . . And you shall make a mercy seat of pure gold, . . . and the cherubim shall have their wings spread upward, covering the mercy seat . . . and you shall put the mercy seat on top of the ark, and in the ark you shall put the testimony which I shall give to you. And there I will meet with you. (Excerpts from Ex. 25:10–22 NAS)

This place was sanctified. Orders were clear. No one was to touch the ark. It is important that we grasp the holiness of this object which was sanctified. No one could touch it. God's orders!

In the time of David, the ark was to be transported. Careful instructions were to be followed to the letter. Yet enroute,

> Uzzah put forth his hand to the ark of God, and took hold of it, for the oxen stumbled. And the anger of the Lord was kindled against Uzzah; and God smote him there for his error; and there he died by the ark of God. (2 Sam. 6:6-7)

The instructions were that *no one could touch it*. Then like a crisis, there arose a human reason to touch it. The oxen pulling the cart stumbled. Naturally Uzzah steadied it. It was an instinctive reaction to not let it fall. He was protecting it. All of his personal reasoning did not change God's commandment.

Skeptics will be quick to judge God for His action in killing Uzzah. That was harsh. Did not God have the time to listen to the reasons? The carnal mind enjoys developing a believer's book of excuses. *Excuses never get the attention of God.* Uzzah was struck dead for one reason—he touched something that belonged to God. Something that had been declared holy.

There are many things in the Bible that were sanctified. To help us visually picture this solemn teaching, imagine a gold box that will be representative of what I call the treasury of the Lord. In this gold box we will place things that are sanctified to God—offerings that are not optional when we enlist in His service.

The first thing to be deposited in the treasury is our tithe. One tenth of everything, God said, is sanctified. The Bible tells us that the tithe is holy.

I readily need to remind myself just what holy means. It means sanctified. Sanctified means set apart for God's use . . . the first tenth. People do not always understand that if they give just a tenth to God, that is not tithing unless it is the *first tenth*. Human reasoning likes to debate this with God. With the thoughts that as soon as the bills are paid, or when the family catches up from a vacation, or the braces are paid for . . . then it will be easier to tithe. We are told to give the first tenth, not the second or the third tenth. The first tenth is holy.

In that gold box your mind constructed, place the first tenth of your income. When you do, it has been placed in the treasury of the Lord. It is holy. Ask yourself now, Whose is this one-tenth? The answer is positive. *The first tenth is the Lord's.*

It is not uncommon at the end of the month when it appears there is "too much month for the money" that, after depositing that tithe into God's treasury, someone is having a problem meeting a house payment. Surely it must be possible to reach back into that gold box and use the tithe for the house payment with full knowledge and personal guarantee that it will be repaid.

The "Uzzah reasoning" in all of us tends again to open a believer's book of excuses. The reality of the ark was that everything put inside of it was holy. The tithe is holy—set apart and sanctified. Even though it appears the apple cart of our finances is about to be upset, as was the cart that carried what God had proclaimed holy, it is *never* to be touched. We never have a right to take out of the box what we have put in for the Lord. It is His. It is holy. It is sanctified. It is set apart for God's use—God's alone. What must get our attention is that it is just as sacreligious for us to touch the tithe we put into the treasury of the Lord, for any reason, as it was for Uzzah to touch the ark of the covenant. It is God's.

There are other things in the Bible that were also sanctified. One was the firstborn of every animal, which was to be given to God. It was sanctified and it was holy. Again, in your mind, take a piece of paper to represent a deed to the things that are sanctified, and put it into the treasury of the Lord.

May I touch that deed? May I mortgage it for just a short time? Never! It is set apart for that which is God's. Once it goes into the box, it is sealed and cannot be touched. In biblical times, when there was famine and the people got hungry for steaks, it would have been easy to reach in and butcher that animal set apart. *No way!* It was set apart.

Another thing sacred in the Bible accounts, and something that was sanctified, was the firstborn male child. In the time of the patriarchs there was no house of God. No church. No tabernacle or temple. The people worshiped in their homes, gathered under the leadership of the father of the house who had priestly rights. His firstborn male child was trained in the ways of a priest, and if the father died, the child inherited those rights. The firstborn son then carried on the duties until the more formal priesthood came along and God ordained the blessed and put His anointing upon a priestly tribe.

Another thing that the Word says is sanctified is the Bible itself. It is holy unto God. That means we cannot profanely touch it. We cannot change it. We all had better be very careful with the translations we make from it. We have to be cautious to use it in context. "Thy word I have treasured in my heart, that I may not sin against Thee" (Ps. 119:11). We are admonished that we cannot change what was inspired by God or what is sacred and untouchable. We put that Bible into the Lord's treasury and cannot misuse it. "For truly I say to you, until heaven and earth pass away, not the smallest letter or stroke shall pass away from the law, until all is accomplished" (Matt. 5:18 NAS).

In the Old Testament the Holy of Holies was sacred. The ark of the covenant was sacred. And the tenth is sanctified. It is holy. It is set apart by God for God.

The reason I desired to write this book was to share essentials that have become mandatory in my life. The church has often failed in teaching these truths. Therefore people are robbed, God is robbed, and a dastardly sin is committed.

There are those who feel tithing and the sacredness of the treasury of the Lord are optional issues in life. I have found that not true. The Bible says: "Therefore to him who knoweth to do good and doeth it not, to him it is sin" (James 4:17). The old historic Westminster Catechism stated, "Sin is any want of conformity unto or transgression of the Law of God."

God's people are responsible for what God declares, whether the sin is committed or omitted. Through these teachings we learn a greater reverence for God and His department of the treasury. As individuals we are accountable.

THE GREATEST ABILITY IS ACCOUNTABILITY

There is another story in God's Book found in the fourth chapter of Genesis, which says, "Adam knew Eve his wife, and she conceived, bare Cain . . . And she bare his brother Abel." From Sunday school we remember the sequence. Abel tithed. Cain did not. The first recorded homicide was committed by one of these brothers because one fellow tithed and the other did not.

Christians must get serious about what belongs in the treasury of the Lord. The first tenth of all income is holy. It is sacred. It is set apart. It belongs to God. The human race fell, the murder was committed, Achan and his family died because they acted as though God was not serious about what was set apart for Him.

Focus again on that imaginary gold box, which now holds what God has stated is holy. We will make another addition to its contents. The Bible says each body is holy.

One of my favorite stories centers around a little Salvation Army girl who stood in front of a department store ringing her bell one Christmas. After a long day she was weary. It was cold outside. She longed to get a cup of hot chocolate, so she left a note on the traditional old black pot, "What will you give for the Master this year?"

An elderly alcoholic walked by and read those words. His heart burned within him, and he reached into his pocket and dropped in a dime. It settled in the pot with its own ring. He started to walk away, but the words lodged in an inner part of his life: "What will you give for the Master this year?" He went back and tossed in a nickel . . . and then his last penny.

When the girl returned from her warm drink, she saw the grizzled old man *sitting in the pot,* the tears pouring down his cheeks, washing him cleaner than he had been for a long time. *He wanted to give the Master his all,* so he gave himself.

That we as individuals should place ourselves in the treasury of the Lord is a gift that brings joy to the heart of God. It is Paul's meaning of presenting ourselves "a living sacrifice, holy and acceptable unto God which is your reasonable service." We are set apart. We are sanctified. We are holy. "For you are a holy people to the Lord your God; the Lord your God has chosen you to be a people for His own possession" (Deut. 7:6 NAS).

My heart longs that this message of being set apart rings, like that Salvation Army bell, into the lives of young people. We need our children to realize their lives and bodies are to be living sacrifices. Lust, liquor, and drugs are not a part of the "set apart."

There are other things that are just as sacred, in addition to what God Himself sanctified. These are things that you make holy when you come to the throne of grace in prayer, and promise that you are giving or giving up something to God. For example, the church is having a missionary conference. One of the members is blessed and pledges a thousand dollars to the mission fund. It was a pledge signed on a card and recorded in the treasury of the Lord. That one thousand dollars becomes holy. It becomes just as holy as a tithe. It has been mentally deposited. It is no longer a possession of the giver. If the giver reneges on that, it is as bad as Uzzah touching the ark of the covenant in the holy of holies, by the mercy seat.

I believe the church needs a revival, the kind that recognizes the holiness of God. One that causes people to pay their bills—not to try to find ways of beating out the creditors. I will never understand why people seek ways to beat God.

This church is His holy temple. Here we sanctify things and make them holy as unto the Lord.

Let me share a personal illustration. For years in this church, God has impressed me to give twenty dollars to the bus ministry on Wednesday nights. I did that for a long time. It was a commitment to God's treasury. Not long ago, I made a large contribution which represented most of my income. I told myself that it would no longer be necessary to give that weekly gift to the bus ministry because of that one large sum. I rationalized that I had established a "credit," and those weekly offerings could be "charged" against it. Then God nudged me with a reminder that I had made a commitment that as long as I was pastor of Phoenix First Assembly, I would give twenty dollars of money each week to the bus program. My pledge had been sanctified. It was holy.

In the treasury of the Lord there are the tithes. God made them holy. In the treasury of the Lord there are the offerings. God made the offering holy first, but people made them holy when they dedicated them unto God.

Grasp the truth, that which we make holy is just as sanctified as what God made holy. We dare not rob God.

Ananias and Sapphira had been bystanders when Barnabas sold a piece of land he owned in Cyprus. He gave the profits to God. The people of the church cheered. It was furthering the gospel, and they were pleased. So Ananias and Sapphira decided to sell a part of their land, and maybe the people would cheer for them. But there was an unhappy twist of events. When they decided to sell the land *for the Lord's work*, at that moment it was no longer their property. It became holy. It was deposited into the treasury of the Lord. Then they decided not to give it all, after it already had been set apart. God was displeased.

They held back from God "with full knowledge." Within an interval of three hours, both were dead. They had touched that which was the tithe. That which was set apart.

Many make a promise to God that they will win souls. It is a moment of commitment, made at an altar or in the sanctuary of an individual's heart. This promise goes into the treasury of the Lord. It becomes set apart—holy. It is placed right there beside the Holy of Holies. Right beside the mercy seat in the ark of the covenant, surrounded by the golden candlesticks.

People make a vow for full-time Christian service. It is secured. Then something changes. People have a way of going in and out of God's service as if it were a revolving door. What was promised to God is sacred. He does not forget. The excuses for breaking the commitment come easily. Comments like I forgot, I got busy, my family, I did not realize what I was doing that night, or I did not understand the cost to my life. The Bible says we are without excuse. "The gifts and calling of God are without repentance."

What about the times there is a fresh challenge to pray and read the Word? The decision is made, "I will read the Bible and pray every morning for thirty minutes." When that decision is made, it is deposited into God's treasury. Then what happens? "And the cares of this world, and the deceitfulness of riches, and the lusts of other things enter in, choke the word, and it becomes unfruitful" (Mark 4:19). Unfruitful and unprofitable? Sad commentaries on those who place valid things into the box that God made holy.

Several years ago a man came up to me after a service. He was the kind of a fellow who led with his chin—you knew he had something on his mind. He said to me, "Brother Barnett, I don't have to come to church on Wednesday night because it is not holy. Sunday was set aside as holy unto God, but not Wednesday night!"

I looked him straight in the eyes, and said to him that in my church Wednesday night is holy. Why? Because years ago I got down on my knees and said to God that I would do my best with His help and grace to be in church every Wednesday night. I placed Wednesday night right beside Sunday in importance. It became holy to me.

I desire that pastors and their people take a new stand for stability. In an age where everyone goes wherever the wind blows, we need to solidify some biblical truths. I see, as I travel around the country, fad and fancies and new programs in abundance. I do not see a lot of stability. If we do not hold a hard line of God's "holy and acceptable will," how will the next generation and the ones to follow have a stable foundation? How can we be certain that faith will flourish on the earth? I will tell you how. By being in church on Sundays and Wednesday nights. By being consistent.

There are people in my church who have been here more than twenty years. They have sung in the choir and taught Sunday school. They are deacons. These people provide the stability a church needs. When kids come home from college, they see familiar faces. Their kids have the same Sunday school teachers. They know the pastors. There is love forming—across the generations. Christianity will become self-propagating. We need to give this kind of stability to our kids.

The world does not seek to stabilize the kids. Scandals are rampant. Fraud and deceit are the norm in this old world. There are even credibility problems among the clergy. Politically, we have seen elections where candidates pull out because of misconduct. Others are forced out for ethical reasons.

The church has to be the rock-solid source of truth. "Therefore my beloved brethren, be ye steadfast, unmovable, always abounding in the work of the Lord, forasmuch as ye know that your labor is not in vain in the Lord" (1 Cor. 15:58). If as parents and church people, we live by our word and our vows, and the young people watch us deposit in God's treasury what is His, and we *leave it there*, we will see unprecedented church growth.

How many times have you promised God that you would study the Bible and read it through in a year? What you did when you made that promise was to place the time it took to read God's Word alongside the tithe, beside the Savior, beside the Bible. When you gave it, you gave it to God.

At Phoenix First Assembly the challenge of the bus kids is exciting and exhilarating to many. When they see these kids pile up on our platforms in heaps, and hear them sing and quote Scripture and say that their lives have been turned around, we have a lot of people making commitments to work in that ministry. I believe they are sincere. I am convinced at that moment it was a personal treasury bill that could be banked on. But then something happens. The excitement wears off, and because of that, a bus may sit idle when it could be packed with youngsters who could spill out from the platform into the aisles, if only that holy, set-apart commitment had been secured.

I have watched the wheelchairs come in, and have seen people visibly moved. They know of loved ones who are infirm and crippled who need to be at church. A decision is made to become involved with the wheelchair ministry and bring the loved ones. Then the commitment dies, like a forgotten check placed in the bottom drawer of a never-used desk. Useless to both parties—God and humankind.

A pastor told one of my workers that Pastors' School challenged him to buy a bus. He did. They started filling it up. Then the price of gasoline went up. There was a slight altercation. The cost of bus insurance went up, and today the bus is covered with dust, parked nonproductively, in the lot of a church declining in membership. When the price of running the bus went up, the commitment went down. What was holy had been desecrated. God cannot be pleased.

We started our bus program when the gas shortage was in full force. We do not get into or out of ministries because of exterior circumstances. We move because we have gone for a challenge. Another opportunity to save souls, to heal hurts and to meet needs. Those churches who dare touch the "ark" that God constructed may brag their finances are better, since their buses were sold, but I would be fearful of God's assessment of the situation. We never have the right to reach into His treasury and pull out what has been put in, in the name of the Lord.

There is something else that I believe goes into the treasury of the Lord. That is the day a man and woman come down the aisle and pledge their troth to one another. It was for better or worse and for richer or poorer, in sickness and health, and the two became one. Each vowed they would love the other, stick together, and grow in grace and in a knowledge of the Lord. The two had become "one"—but the separation happened when they questioned "which one?"

One day one spouse decides he or she just doesn't love the other anymore. It's all over. They are not compatible. There are too many differences. "What God has joined together let no man put asunder" has fallen on deaf and selfish ears. I am convinced that whatever caused that love in the first place can usually be rekindled. For what is in the Lord's treasury is holy.

While it would be my great desire as a pastor to see marriages endure, I am aware that sin and circumstances can dissolve unions. I also know that God accepts us where we are and is the God of a second chance. His ever-widening circle of love encompasses *all* who come to Him.

At a former church location, I remember a pastor who left his wife because of his infidelity and sin. He was fired from his church and felt like a spiritual outcast. He found his way into our Third Street building, and told me of the separation. He was the discouraged portrait of a fallen leader.

I told him he had made a vow. God was going to hold him to it. It was and is sacred. It is dangerous to break it. I will never forget watching him run to the altar, slide to his knees, and weep. He stood up as if he had determined to keep the vow in the treasury, and drove home. He waited in the driveway until his wife returned. He confessed his sin and asked forgiveness. They had a lot of things to solve, but the Spirit of God worked in their hearts, and they renewed a commitment. Today he is involved in a great church for the glory of the Lord.

One of the most precious gifts that goes into the treasury of the Lord is our children. There is the day a parent or parents stand on the platform, proud and eager to dedicate their bundle to the Lord. Believe me, that is not just a simple occasion in my life. First of all, I cannot save that child. Baby dedication is awesome, for in that step the parents are committing themselves to bringing up the child in the nurture and admonition of the Lord. That day is registered in heaven.

That commitment means having those children in church and Sunday school, teaching them the Word at home, praying with them at night, living the precepts: "Then teach them the statutes of the laws, and make known to them the way in which they are to walk, and the work they are to do" (Ex. 18:20). If those children are not taught, you have taken that which is holy, set in your hands, and not treated the dedication as something that was sacred.

A lot of people feel I am too intense in the ministry. Most books would share the lighter side of life, the safe and comfortable areas. My life has never been very normal. Lots of people have said I am against too many things. They are right. I am against *all wrong!* It would be a whole lot more convenient to take it easier, but years ago I made a vow to God.

I was thirteen years old. I had been in a congregation where everyone was excited and rejoicing that Bill Baker, the handsome basketball player, came to the front and announced he was going into the ministry. You should have heard the cheers and thrills. He would make it. He did!

Then Ray Thomas, an outstanding baseball player, came. He announced to the church that he was going into the ministry, and everyone was ecstatic. With these great athletes the church would surely survive.

On another Sunday, a sixty-nine-pound kid walked the same aisle, and when they announced that God had called little Tommy into the ministry, no one got too excited. (Someone dared think that the angels folded their wings and wept!) But I remember kneeling and making a promise: "Oh, God, I may not be tall and handsome like old Bill Baker, and I may not have all the abilities of Ray Thomas, but I can give you something they can't give you—and that's sixty-nine pounds of Tommy Barnett."

I made a vow with God that night—a vow to God till death do us part—or brings us together. I tiptoed up to His treasury and deposited my life. I knew I could never touch it again. It was His, for His service and at His command.

The world is full of people who steal from the Lord's treasury. People who have said to God, "If You will heal my baby, I will serve You. . . . If You will get me out of Vietnam, I will serve You. . . . If I just don't get caught this once in my sin, I will never do it again. . . . If, as a pastor, I can just find another church, I will serve God and the people with my whole heart. . . . If . . . If . . ." And graciously God says, "If my people which are called by My name, shall humble themselves and pray and turn from their wicked ways, then I will hear" (2 Chron. 7:14).

You may even want to lay this book aside right now, and if you have anything of God's you have taken, just put it back in His treasury and leave it there.

We do not have to close a chapter with the deadly results of Uzzah, Achan, or Ananias and Sapphira. God is so good. He is gracious. He is merciful. If we draw nigh to Him, He draws nigh to us. We are the ones who move away from His everlasting care. His invitation for change is open-ended:

> For a brief moment I forsook you, But with great compassion I will gather you. In an outburst of anger I hid My face from you for a moment; But with everlasting lovingkindness I will have compassion on you, says the Lord, your Redeemer. (Isa. 54:7, 8)

The head of the United States Treasury Department is called the secretary of the treasury. He is a respected person who is responsible, honorable, and accountable. We, too, have been given a magnificent opportunity to guard that which we have placed into the treasury of the Lord. It is sanctified. It is holy. Untouchable! Irreplaceable—except for the grace of God. Holy, sanctified deposits earn compound *eternal* interest!

11

The Many Faces of Pro-Vision

ONE OF the overasked questions at Pastors' School is, "Where do you get the money for all of your programs?" The question takes on various shapes and intensity. One pastor from Idaho may say his limited population would never support this type of ministry. Another from one of America's high-density cities may respond that neither would his church of over a thousand members. They are simply not rich. Many disbelieve that growth produces funding. They have been taught the opposite is true—that funding precedes growth.

Phoenix First Assembly believes that the common dilemma of church "red ink" is usually a result of not accepting the biblical mandate of the New Testament church, which did win souls, heal hurts, and meet needs. Finances become available when the principles of Jesus Christ are heeded. That introduces a revolution of love, and money is released.

I was convinced that when I had only seventy-six members in my first congregation in Davenport, Iowa, that within that house of God there were people and funds to move toward five hundred. When I had five hundred, I again found within God's house the people and finances for one thousand. Now the growth continues in astounding proportions and with sustaining resources.

The faces that portray God's *supply* of the financial needs are as diversified as the faces in the parking lot on a Sunday morning. They include all strata of socioeconomic profiles, including my staff and me. All are givers with the unusual dimension of *giving with joy!*

I have found that one layperson has the capability to change a church. That person can redirect the atmosphere, build excitement, and create the energy needed to move that church into great things for God. Such an individual is Craig Smith, thirty-five years old, and today his corporation is worth millions of dollars. He sits on the sofa in my office, relaxed in style but hypermotivated in his personal desire to be one of the financial bases of his church.

Life has not always been so relaxed for SwissAmerica's founder and president. He had been a Christian, but was not taught issues of righteousness and holiness. There was a time in his life when marijuana, cocaine, and other evil forces were common. One day he was drawn to visit me. He had made a new commitment to the Lord. He shared that he wanted to do something big for God. He was concerned about the youth of the land, and dedicated to working on ways to bring kids to church and keeping them there. After having leaned in the wrong direction, he was ready for a new route. I showed him around our facility, and shared some of my dreams for a new educational building, prayer chapel, and expansion of ministries.

Craig felt a tug in his heart toward this great church, so he announced that he was going to give one million dollars! I had heard such statements many times in the past, and let the remark go by. It did not go by Craig Smith. He had no idea where the sum would ever come from, but he wrote the pledge indelibly across his heart.

One Sunday the sermon had been presented on getting a vision. It was said that the people should go home and write the vision down for their individual lives or for a company or corporation. The words from Habakkuk had been shared: "Write the vision, and make it plain upon the tables, that he may run that readeth it. For the vision is yet for an appointed time, but at the end it shall speak, and not lie: though it tarry, wait for it; because it will surely come, it will not tarry" (Hab. 2:2, 3).

Craig was the kind of eager believer who would sit on the edge of the pew and drink in the words that were poured forth. Craig understood Jeremiah's heart toward God: "Thy words were found, and I did eat them; and Thy word was unto me the joy and rejoicing of mine heart" (Jer. 15:16).

What he wrote down that Sunday after church made no sense. The improbability factor was off the charts. Being pragmatic, he knew it would take "twenty-plus miracles" for his vision to be accomplished. He tucked it in his Bible, and kept an invisible recording sheet close to his mind.

As a coin and precious metal dealer he became willing, not just to contribute his coins—but to give of himself. He started helping in the prisons and was growing in the Lord. One day in his haste, he left his Bible on his car and started to drive away. The wind swept most of the contents of the Book down the street, but amazingly his written vision of months before withstood the air turbulence. Little did he know then that soon he would be in the vortex of a personal tornado.

On a business-as-usual day, sixty treasury agents, IRS people, stormed his offices with guns and an incriminating subpoena demanding that he produce all his records. The hysteria of his staff was frightening. It is difficult to understand why an agent could not have called or simply come to ask for the records. They were readily available. He would have been willing to comply. The incident resembled a B-grade movie, though the leading character was far more dramatic.

More unbelievable to Craig was the shock in his spiritual being as to just what God was doing. He had recently told God that he wanted to "help Him out—to give a million dollars." Then he became a victim of conspiracy that appeared set up. As officers read him his rights, he contemplated an uncertain future. Today he realizes that God has His way of testing a man and refining him by fire. Possibly God needed to know for certain what his future relationship would be to wealth.

The church has a Joash box for making special gifts. The Joash concept in the Old Testament was a means of giving special gifts. Wonderful stories come from those who faithfully contribute in this way to the Lord. Craig was told about that box during his trying times. He also was becoming cognizant that he should tithe from his business as well as from his personal accounts. A revelation like this stunned not only Craig but his accountants. During the time the IRS was involved in his life, his resources were very limited. But he had determined to give. The first check written on the business was about one dollar. Almost hesitantly, he gave it to me. He did not want me to see the amount.

Then he stood in the Joash lines each week with his modest gift and burning desire to see buildings built and God glorified on the church grounds.

Craig Smith shares that he is not into building per se, but in Arizona you don't meet outdoors in football stadiums when the thermometer hits 113 degrees. People need a place for worship and teaching. He believed he was destined to become one of the financial architects of God's building program. Arrogant? Never!

Craig's problems were resolved. He felt the strength of church support and never wavered in his giving.

Even in trying times, the checks deposited into the Joash box got larger each week. Opportunities opened up. Miracles began to happen, more than "twenty-plus miracles" that he conceded were needed when he made the commitment to God to give the first million. Today he confesses he wishes his faith had been greater than that initial pledge. He is convinced "according to your faith, be it unto you!"

Businessmen going through deep waters came to him for counsel. He started a radio program called "World Economic Perspective." It airs on one hundred seventeen stations and is syndicated into over eight hundred programs. Through the program he shares a biblical perspective with listeners.

Why are Craig Smith and his SwissAmerica Corporation giving upwards of eight thousand dollars a week to the church these days? God has been faithful. *"Him that honoreth me I will honor."* The business is growing in gargantuan proportions. Other precious metal and rare coin houses continue to seek his advice. He has seminars that break into times to witness to God's glory. His brokers may witness over the telephone. His life and business are centered in God's business. His "recorded" dream came to fruition: *"Though it tarry, wait for it!"*

Craig recently reminded me of the time I preached on "Quit Saying It Is Too Good To Be True." For when you have asked for something and He gives it to you, *it is true*—and it is God giving it to you. "All that we have comes from the Lord, and we give it out of His hand" (Dutch translation of 1 Chron. 29:14).

Each month since Craig started the tithing checks, his business has increased. Miracles are normal. It is phenomenal what God will do when you trust Him. Never has he tithed expecting God to return to him anything. Never has he said, "God, here is one hundred dollars. It is all I have, please send it back one-hundred-fold." Rather, "I give because of who God is and what He has done for me. I give because Pastor Barnett is my hero, and he taught me the joy of how Jesus gave. If Christians love God, they have to love to give—time, money, and themselves. God does not allow us to steal from Him."

Craig now knows that a man can have everything, but if he is not a giver, he cannot experience life's ultimate joy. He smilingly admits he does not understand the economy of God, but he has figured out this much. God must get "tickled" when His children give, and then He tickles them by giving to them and letting them tickle Him again! Craig dearly loves the Lord. At times the presence of God and what He means in his life is overwhelming. He shares how loving and caring and correcting God has been. He underlines the privilege of being in a church where he can see growth results of his giving. Giving from *need* and giving from excess. Giving not until it hurts, but until it feels good so that souls are saved and people helped.

He tells how Pastor Jack Wallace and I kept him going by our trust in him and our encouragement during the dark days. We constantly reminded him not to give up because Jesus never gave up. To hang in there! That tomorrow would be a better day! I would tap him on the shoulder, and in fatherly fashion learned from my own dad years ago, tell him, "It's going to be okay!" And it was okay!

What does this church mean to Craig Smith and his family? It is the center of their lives. Especially meaningful was an incident which occurred recently. One of his two daughters (ages seven and nine) had been playing Nintendo. There is a program that involves a perceived death angel. There was some discussion as to the reality of there being such a thing as a death angel. The discussion was concluded when his nine year old stated that even if there was a death angel, it would not matter. She would simply "plead the blood over the doorpost of their house, and all would be well!" What is that kind of teaching and assurance of God worth? To Craig Smith, everything he has—today and tomorrow. A true portrait of uninhibited, visionary giving.

Watching the example of giving was "caught" by me more than taught to me when I was young. I watched my father give to the church, not just a part of his meager savings, but all of it. When I was a little boy, my parents pastored a small Texas church. There I observed my dad give up his entire retirement account. He had started out by trying to teach the people to give. Finally, as an example, my dad said he would give one thousand dollars. The people began to respond. Then he added another one thousand dollars. Subsequently he felt God was saying give it all, so the last one thousand dollars of a three thousand dollar savings account went to the house of God. Because I saw my dad do it, the imprint is forever on my own bank account.

A pastor must do more than feed his sheep. A pastor with a heart is called to sacrifice. Because the return is always so great, I would like to delete "sacrifice" from the dictionary. It is difficult for people to understand my visionary heart—I would die for my vision. I would also give to my vision "good measure, pressed down, overflowing!"

When the new sanctuary was being built in Phoenix, I had asked the congregation for the greatest possible investment for God's house. I encouraged them to give the best gift ever, the largest they had made. I began searching my own heart and finances.

When I was young, my folks had given me a mutual fund with a value of about $8,700. Since pastors often sign off Social Security, this was to be a trust fund. My dad admonished me, "Son, give a lot to God, but not this trust, this is your retirement—someday it will be a fortune."

Through the years I have added to the fund, bringing its value to about $160,000. It was not enough to build the building, nor even really start the building, but it was the best gift my family could give to set the pace for the congregation to follow.

When leaving Davenport, Marja and I had a thirteen thousand dollar residual from our home sale. It was used to purchase a small piece of land in the desert. Through Arizona land appreciation, the value skyrocketed when a Jack Nicklaus Golf Course was planned for that area. The value exceeded $350,000. We were overwhelmed.

Now money truly became a family matter, for the children's education had to be considered as well as retirement. Marja and the children and I met as a group, and it was discussed at length. It was Marja who said, "Did God tell you to give it?" I chose not to answer, for I knew if I had said yes, they would have voted that way. The vote was taken without my response . . . and it was unanimous. *Give it ALL to the Lord!*

When I drive to the office or go by the church and see my investment, I never see lost equity or demolished savings. I see souls, little bus kids, families restored, alcoholics set free, and ministry expansion. Costly? Perhaps. But with enduring, everlasting dividends.

Like ripples from a pebble tossed in a brook, the waves of these gifts are continually felt. A "snowbird" from the north, who came to Phoenix for the winter with his wife, visited Phoenix First Assembly the day I gave the property. The visiting guest vowed in his heart to someday respond by giving his best gift also. Three years later when this man, still not a member of the Phoenix church sold some property, he brought a check for seventy thousand dollars—in appreciation for a pastor who practiced what he preached.

Ed Unicum, a member of the church's EPIC team, called one evening, wanting to see me at a local Denny's. I was busy with my boys in basketball, but later my family and I met Mr. Unicum and his son Mark for a time of fellowship. The Unicums brought a check for a quarter of a million dollars! They wanted to see my expression!

Stories like this could fill another book. These are a few of the encouragements representative of many whose gifts, large and small, provide for this work. I love to talk about EPIC people—my sounding board on financial and business matters. Brilliant, visible men like Fred Boulineau, Craig Smith, Lu Warner combined with Jack Carey, Michael Clifford, Dave Friend, Allan Mayer, Ed Unicum, Bill Tathum, Jr., and Charley Graves. Charley sold his business some years ago to be a volunteer consultant on financial matters. Most of these names are household words in Phoenix. They would prefer being called people who love God, and have committed themselves and their substance into His treasury.

I am grateful that God keeps His promise of pro-vision. Whom He calls, He enables in unexpected ways.

Offerings at Phoenix First Assembly are made in differing dimensions. A child puts in a stick of gum "to Jesus," a little gray-haired lady slips in a piece of jewelry. A bag lady drops in food stamps. Coins are untied from the corner of a handkerchief. The last paper money in a billfold is released into the passing plate for the Lord. A mountain of offering envelopes are a tribute to the faithful who have learned what is holy and sanctified to the Lord.

As Craig Smith says, "God is tickled." We know that He is never unmindful of gifts—large or small, they are all counted for righteousness.

C. S. Lewis wrote that

> God the Creator has no needs. However, man as the creature has needs. And one of man's greatest needs is to be needed. God in His great love for us has met man's needs including his need to be needed. Thus allowing man to be a necessary contributing party in God's plan of salvation for man. (C. S. Lewis Library, Wheaton College, Wheaton, IL)

Those who give to the Lord are allowed to be participants or co-laborers with God. What a privilege! What an honor! To be able to put tithe and offering into the Lord's treasury and to let it be recorded in an eternal account.

Another widely recognized face of pro-vision is my dear friend Allan Mayer of Oscar Mayer Packing fame. Grandson of the founder and oldest of his father's five sons, Allan is exemplary of a loving theology of giving.

He illustrates to the world the command that we are not to "lay up treasures on earth," but to "lay up treasures in heaven." In Philippians 4, the apostle Paul shares his conviction about eternal awards, saying that gifts to ministry were not as essential to him as they were to those who were giving the gifts. For from the giving, eternal accounts will abound and be multiplied. Therefore, God is glorified.

God *is* glorified through Allan as he shares his story at Pastors' School and with the congregation. He is free to say he was born into abundance. He possessed all the seemingly wonderful things that strong balance sheets can obtain: homes, custom automobiles, pools, tennis courts, and boats. Things that surround the rich and famous. Yet amidst the plenty there was lack. To satisfy the lack and fill the emptiness, he turned to alcohol, medications, and things the world calls pleasure. He had visited many mainline churches. He was always welcomed, but the "light" he sought was missing.

Allan had been touched by Jesus' words: "Come unto me all you who are weary and heavy laden, and I will give you rest" (Matt. 11:28). He sought that kind of rest. During the time his young daughter was diagnosed with a brain tumor, he came to faith through reading Kathryn Kuhlman's book on divine healing. He accepted Jesus Christ. The child got well.

Among visits to churches, he came to Phoenix First Assembly at its Third Street location. Here he began to feel that fullness of Christ he was looking for. Here he recognized this was not a church for social purposes, but for the work of the Lord. Allan has never stopped coming. He appreciates the reality that everyone is welcome. There are no distinctions among the people. The open arms of the Lord are extended to *all* who come. It reflects Jesus' invitation, "Whosoever will may come." Allan appreciates the great participation of all the people. It is a center for caring. A place of refreshing, and one where people grow.

Allan explains his love for the church is two-fold. The wonderful preaching and teaching build people. It is also a place where people can become involved and give their time and abilities and service to help humanity—a duality that is worthy of support.

Those who know Allan Mayer say they have never known such a godly man, that he truly walks with God. They have never heard him say a derogatory word about anyone. He dearly loves his family, and possesses a tender heart for the lost.

Allan is quick to buy a semi-truckload of food for the poor if the pantry is empty. He is a major contributor to the benevolent fund. He purchased the magnificent stained glass window above the baptistry and lavishly gives of his love and prayers to people. He is often found setting tables for the needy when the church will feed up to fifteen thousand. It has not been enough just to share the finances; he is a physical part of what he gives. As he moves among the people, serving, caring, and loving, he walks unnoticed—except in the book of God's remembrance.

Still involved with the Oscar Mayer foundation, here is a man who is a biblical portrait of pro-vision. His heart is toward God. Articulate and caring, he may be speaking for a businesspersons' Christian organization or purchasing bicycles for bus kids. He blesses the church, personally and financially.

At the beginning of this chapter the pastors posed the question, "Where do you get the money for all of your programs?" The answer comes clearly and boldly. People give when they see results. They give when their hearts are touched. The Old Testament writers told about those who came "whose hearts were made willing." How? By being touched with what touches God. "God loveth a cheerful giver" (2 Cor. 9:7). "Cheerful" was originally translated as "hilarious." God loves *hilarious* givers.

Businesspeople want a return on their investment. They are bottom-line oriented. It is not surprising they have reacted to the recurring question at Phoenix First Assembly of "What is in your house?" and willingly deposited more than the tithe and more than their offering, *hilariously,* into the treasury of the Lord.

Combined with the gifts of all faithful members, the carefully audited financial statements are a tribute and a model for total spiritual accountability.

12

Staff Pro-Vision

WHEN IS a church big enough? How much staff does it take to meet the pastoral needs of a large church? Interesting questions with surprising answers.

I remember a woman who loved God coming to me asking, "Pastor, isn't our church big enough?"

She was aware that for some time we had been praying for her unsaved son, so I asked her, "If your son came to our church and accepted Christ as his Savior, do you think we would have room for one more?"

Bowing her head, she answered her own question. "Yes. We would."

Churches earnestly seek to meet the needs of a woman wanting her son to come to faith. The method used is almost universal—bring in an evangelist or place special emphasis on the lost, preach to them and hopefully some will be saved. It then becomes the responsibility of the clergy to care for the ever-increasing flock. If the church grows so much that it becomes impossible to marry or bury or otherwise take care of the parishioners, the usual denominational order of the day is to hire another staff member. After all, staff people are paid to do the job. If people continue to come into the church, and the pressures increase, another staff person is hired and soon, if the church isn't careful, there will be a church full of "hireds."

At our church we have only eleven on our pastoral staff, and we do that on purpose. We do not want to take the work and put it into the hands of the paid staff. We want to keep it in the work of the ministry—which is the people. My job is to encourage, motivate, review, and challenge. The people's job is to do the work of the ministry. So as pastor, I minister to the ministers. The people go out where the sinners are and bring them in.

One of my recurring themes is Acts 2:47. "And the Lord added to the church daily such as should be saved." If Scripture is inspired, and we know it is, should not a church bring in 365 converts a year? I call it my "one-a-day brand of Christianity!"

How did that New Testament church accomplish that goal? They did it "in the Temple and in the villages." Yet today churches have tried to accomplish this growth only by copying the first half—"in the Temple" (church). The only way people are added daily is if the members are winning souls daily in the temple *and* in the villages. A pastor or his paid staff's personal evangelism is not sufficient.

It amazes me that surveys conclude that more than 80 percent of the admitted unconverted will not go to church under any circumstances. Since our Lord is not willing that any should perish, it is logical that we should go to them.

The twentieth-century program of evangelism has been built on the philosophy that if we build a beautiful building, at a good location, the unchurched will come. Yet studies of the one hundred fastest-growing churches in America revealed location has the least bearing on growth. Nowhere in the Bible does it tell the unsaved to go to church. Because we, the church, have been commanded by God's Word to "go into the highway and hedges and compel them to come in that My house might be filled."

This philosophy begins with the pastor. He is the example. That is why I live with the imperative to win souls. Next I teach the people to be soul-winners. Most are surprised on Sunday mornings I preach to the Christians—up until the last five minutes. I am always training, encouraging and developing soul-winners.

In my early ministry I encouraged churches to be evangelistic. Now I go back to the same churches and encourage them to be soul-winning churches. There is a major difference. In an evangelistic church we go out and invite all the unsaved, and the preacher preaches. The problem with that is the church needs a persuasive preacher. In the soul-winning church, the pastor is the trainer. He does not have to be a powerhouse, a great orator or entertainer. He sends the ministers (his congregation) out, and they minister and then bring the people to the house of God. The evangelistic emphasis is crusades; the soul-winning emphasis conserves and reproduces. The Bible calls the ministers or soul-winners "trees." I believe if the trees are in good shape, one just has to shake them and the fruit falls to the ground!

It is said that *prayer* releases the work of God, *praise* releases the presence of God, and the *Word* releases the power of God. So when I am asked the question about when a church is big enough, I have to reply, "When everyone in our city has accepted Christ. Then and only then is the church big enough and the required prayer, praise, and preaching of the Word accomplished its mission."

The pastor of that growing New Testament church needs support staff. Like the pastor, they are called to encourage and challenge the people within the same priorities. That is why I am a strong advocate of homegrown staff, and why most of Phoenix First Assembly's staff has come from within our church or through my teaching.

EXPLOITS SHOULD BE THE RULE, NOT THE EXCEPTION

To do exploits there must be a vision. The staff needs to share that vision and be willing to die with the pastor for it. The staff is then united in the plan of operation. If the goal is to win souls, they must be soul-winners. They must possess proven commitment to the pastor, the people, and to their area of responsibility. Then I am willing to give them great autonomy to do what God has placed in their hearts. My staff is very aware that there is a price to be paid for this kind of commitment, whether they are paid staff or cherished volunteer staff.

In our denomination there have traditionally been two camps. One says, "Let God do the work," and the other says, "God won't do anything for us that we can do for ourselves." I have never believed in that division. The truth is, both are right. D. L. Moody put it another way: "*Work like it depends on you, pray like it depends on God.*" But work and pray we must. The commitment is essential. Programs alone will not build a church, but if the philosophy is "daily people are added," there will be no limit to the church's growth possibility.

With that background I want to share some of my wonderful staff. These people are committed to me but most of all, committed to the Lord and the work of the Lord. Two, Keith Buchanan and Alvin Booher you have met in other chapters.

Keith Buchanan has faithfully served for ten years. His media abilities have been sought by the professionals. He pioneered special effects such as lasers, fog, and enhanced wire-flying. At Christmas he lights the pageants to bring out every detailed nuance. In the children's toy shop scene he transfers real baby elephants and llamas, young donkeys, camels, and baby lambs right into the stable in Bethlehem, then illuminates the baby Jesus in true spiritual light. Keith is "Mr. Media" and a valued staff member.

Another valued staff member is, without a doubt, Alvin Booher. As he moves toward the age of ninety, he continues to reshape hospital visitation. He may be the first centenarian on my staff!

In looking for staff, I search for character above talent. I believe if an individual has the character, the talent will follow. Pastors tell me today I have a talent for taking persons who are insignificant and making them outstanding. I prefer turning that statement around. I believe I have the insight to recognize the outstanding, and they themselves move from the insignificance. These folks are often offered large salaries and impressive churches—especially after Pastors' School—but they are committed *today* to this church.

Each of my staff merits a chapter or a book. I would gladly write across that book my gratitude to God for one and all; however, my purpose is to highlight just a glimpse into each heart and ministry as a way to prove that God advances these ministries through staff provision.

Dale Lane is an associate pastor who came to Phoenix by way of Davenport. A treasured asset, his wife Lynn has been my personal secretary. Both of the Lanes are team players, and rejoice in every victory, while not being deterred in the intervals of occasional defeat. Dale directs evangelism and supervises the volunteer lay pastors who are a vital force of the staff. Dale's loyalty is solid, and he's grateful for the example and opportunity to "pull a load" for the glory of God as a co-laborer.

Dale started as part of the bus ministry in Iowa. Now he oversees the ministry, with Mark Lampley at the head. He feels his role is to be "Mr. Associate" and represent my vision and mission. Even as Jethro lifted the arms of Moses, so Dale lifts me with his consistent willingness. He describes his broad responsibility with one of the key verses in his life: "Ye have not chosen me, but I have chosen you, and ordained you, that ye should go and bring forth fruit, and that your fruit should remain" (John 15:16). He agrees with my analogy that he and his staff have "Baptist feet and Pentecostal hearts"—all working in love and through the power of the Holy Spirit.

Those looking for a dream, with the accompanying vision and decisive action to serve God as an adventure, find their way onto Phoenix First Assembly paid staff. Today there are businesspeople working toward being self-supporting, so someday they can work in this common cause of winning souls. The staff knows when they join forces, I do my best to be a loyal, positive leader. Sometimes the staff asks which is my favorite ministry. That is easy to answer . . . it's the one being discussed at that given time!

My dad had a vital bus ministry. In Davenport I followed that example. When it grew too large, I passed it into the hands of a former staff member, Bill Wilson, who was the most unlikely candidate if resumes were the judge. Bill grew up in Florida. His family moved to various cities looking for security. There was none. In Florida his parents were divorced. Soon his father died, and his mother worked in a bar, taking a client home night after night. Bill knew no stability.

A man took an interest in this skinny kid. He helped Bill cope as he matured, and was a caring individual who paid Bill's way to camp, taught him mechanics, and showed him a better way. Later a pastor became meaningful as Bill dedicated his life to the Lord. These people provided the sense of support Bill needed. He went to Bible school and then had opportunities, in simple ways, to share the Lord through prisons and the church. The summer to remember was the one his Florida pastor asked him if he would use a church van to pick up kids for Daily Vacation Bible school. He found kids, not unlike himself, and brought them. Bill soon discovered a numbers difference in Daily Vacation Bible school and Sunday school, which alarmed him. He started neighborhood Bible clubs. The children's ministry expanded.

One day he met me, and our hearts locked. The church in Davenport already had a huge bus ministry. Would Bill's background be an issue on a potential job? My philosophy goes back many years. When God opens a door, I never shut that door. Bill knew about bus ministries and was invited to join the staff. Bill accepted the challenge. Years later following great exploits, Bill's call came to move to one of America's last frontiers—pioneering Sunday schools in the ghettos of Brooklyn. My sons and I recently visited Bill. We were appalled at the impossible conditions surrounding the church: poverty, violence, and illicitness paved the streets. During one winter Bill loaned the buses of his Metro Assembly to the homeless for warmth. On arriving to pick them up, he found them stripped of everything. Yet Bill moves on, having Sunday school somewhere in these critical areas of America every day of the week. *Staff are not chosen from resumes.*

Dale Lane picked up Bill Wilson's mantle in Davenport and carried it to Phoenix. When Dale needed help, Mark Lampley came on the scene. Mark, now a staff person, follows in the profile of his pastor. He loves souls and he lives for his ministry. He is quick to tell other bus ministers, "If you don't love souls, scrap the bus ministry." It is expensive, but it is far more than transportation. It is a means of kids taking the high road to Jesus. Buses are about people reaching people, finding shoes for a kid who has none so he can come to church, and meeting all crises areas within capability. He loves sharing stories of watching those kids change, and joy pour into their desolate lives.

Mark's pocket is filled with stories of little kids who have found Jesus and later been killed or died from the lack of funds to be hospitalized; homes that have turned around and bus kids who today serve great churches. Mark's head is full of future ideas to expand his effectiveness. Nothing is stagnant. Everything points to more souls, more needs, and more buses!

I am sometimes asked where I feel erosion could take place in Phoenix First Assembly. I recognize that a large church becomes a feeding ground for other churches. That is normal. I do not fight it. And although the staff has emerged as leaders, I would never ask them to stay if they felt a call to move on. However, most of them believe they are *strong as individuals,* but *stronger corporately.* Ministering to around twelve thousand-plus per week requires strength.

Lloyd Ziegler is a supermotivated young man. He heads the Master's Commission with zeal, energy, and fast-lane drive. He explains life for his student is not typical of college or trade school. It is "a year for God—one tough assignment!" The Master's Commission is a discipleship training ground that is balanced with evangelism training, designed to equip and develop young people. It helps young people, ages eighteen through thirty-five, during the decisive years of life, to form strong relationships, learn responsibility, and to watch God move in people's hearts and lives. Lloyd says he wants to be viewed as an encourager. He uses that to encourage his young people to have a right relationship with God, with others, and with themselves. This they learn as they work in every facet of the church and encourage others on the way.

Many churches are following Phoenix First Assembly's example, and believe the Master's Commission is the school of the future. For indeed it is an equipping ministry.

Lloyd Ziegler grew up in a pastor's home. He has known me for years. He saw the compassion and decided it was something everyone could have and incorporated the trait in his life.

Lloyd came to Pastors' School and heard of the beginnings of the Master's Commission. Born in the heart of Larry Kerychuk, and later carried on by Carmen Balsamo, the idea took residence. One morning Lloyd called and asked me if there would be a place for him at Phoenix First Assembly. He already knew the ministries well. The morning of that call Carmen Balsamo was out jogging, the picture of health. Returning from the run, he had a heart attack and died, with Larry Kerychuk at his side.

That afternoon, feeling stunned, I called Lloyd back and explained what had transpired. In the economy of God, Lloyd stepped in to fill the vacancy. From the omniscient hand of God, another position was filled without the usual church search.

Lloyd explains that society says to do your own thing. That thought process has invaded many churches. Not his church, for he profiles a staff member who is committed to help fulfill my vision and the Great Commission. How is it done? With his life, his time, and his all, he leads by example. He participates in the events of the church, and even flies as an angel at Christmas. He admits to being short-staffed and overloaded, but he also knows where he is going for God and why the harvest must always be reaped. When Lloyd came on staff I said to him, "Lloyd, be kind. We hire staff members who are kind. That is important."

Might it be easy for some to get a swelled head serving here in one of the largest churches on this continent? Lloyd insists it isn't because many days he knows he has failed a person he couldn't reach or not responded as he should have. While the Master's Commission has gone nationwide, that is not the criterion for success. As Lloyd puts it, "I still have to take care of Sister Jones who has called twice because I forgot to pick up her groceries. My lawn at home has to stay mowed because the neighbors know I represent God. The enormity of daily responsibility is frightening at times. I know that without God I am not going to make it. With God, victory is just around the corner."

Larry Kerychuk "caught" a burden for athletes. He serves as director of a worldwide Pentecostal outreach to Christian professional and collegiate athletes. A former professional football player, he sees athletes as "persons" with many needs, not "personalities." Larry was our neighbor when we first moved to Arizona. One day he spent almost three hours, sitting on the kitchen floor with me, sharing his dream. The realization of that dream came in steps until Athletes International Ministries was formed.

Larry's vision is to reach out to athletes and coaches wherever they are, and no matter what the sport or level of expertise. For these are often the visible people who capture half the American television audience through various forms of athletics.

Portraits of athletes these days are varying. Some are great examples. Others have fallen into drug abuse or become victims of the high price of failing in front of a sports-crazy society. Here is a great segment to be turned to Christ, which ultimately could help reach the world. Phoenix '89 featured Hall of Fame personalities, great wide receivers and coaches, representatives of the Harlem Globetrotters, Dallas Cowboys, Chicago Cubs, Denver Broncos, Los Angeles Raiders, as well as women who have excelled in Olympic and national events.

From 1985 until the 1989 conference, the ministry has become the largest convention of its kind in America. The 1989 assembly honored people like former Dallas Cowboys' coach Tom Landry, coach Kay Yow, Barry Sanders, Clarissa Davis, M. L. Harris, Michael Singleton, and others.

Jeff Peterson came from Bible college to Phoenix First Assembly. He is a strong individual who coordinates the high school and junior high ministries. He is talented and also works with music, counseling, teaching, leading worship, and overseeing many ministries of youth. Jeff is aware that he is serving in a church that is not classified a departmental church. It is an outreach church. There may be overlapping, but there is seldom dissension. When you are winning souls, problems have a way of dissolving into victories. His youth department is focused on outreach. Kids are shown how to witness on the street and how to care for others.

Jeff is known as a faithful young man. Kind, tenderhearted and lovable, with a dry sense of humor, the kids respond to him well. In youth ministry it is difficult to find and maintain a balance. Jeff constantly works on new areas to bring meaning to kids, and to see them walk in the planned power of God. A youth director is criticized if he is overly pious or righteous, and frowned upon if he is flamboyant and comedic. Jeff just moves along in the Spirit of God and watches the fruit fall. He has developed Bible studies on high school campuses, a Teen Awareness program to aid parents, and constantly blesses the church.

Walt and Louene Rattray are another wonderful church couple. Louene is Christian Education Director and oversees the Sunday school program. She is diligent, organized, and committed to the best Christian education available for children. Like her husband, she is an ordained minister and combines all aspects of her educational and ministerial background to meet Sunday school needs. Louene believes *a church with a heart includes a Sunday school with a heart for children*. She believes children should be taught for life change, not just to keep them quiet on a Sunday morning. One of her trademarks is her "Rattray's sacred seven"—her philosophy of ministry.

- Teaching is a calling from God.
- You are first a soul-winner, then a teacher.
- Spirit-filled, power-packed preparation begins early each week.
- Always take time to evaluate.
- Many lessons are "caught" not taught, so model Christ.
- Build self-esteem and value in each student, realizing that Christ sees worth in each person.

- A basic routine offers necessary security, but variety is the spice of life.

She holds to the 2 Timothy 2:19 concept of teaching: "A solid foundation stands firm."

Louene also assists her husband in street ministry. Both love to bless others by sharing "fruit picked" in the Sunday school or in a park, within a coffee house or prison—that is true joy. Louene's Sunday school materials often are printed by a man who came to Christ many years ago while on the street. His assistant came from the park—soon he will be a fine mechanic; now loving God, he will help with the buses after he is released from prison.

Through staff members such as Louene and her dear husband Walt, the impoverished in soul and body are brought to pro-vision. They gain new strength and hope from the one who says, "Fear not, for I am with thee, be thou not dismayed; for I am thy God; I will strengthen thee; yea, I will help thee; yea, I will uphold thee with the right hand of My righteousness" (Isa. 41:10).

Jack Wallace directs the Watchman Ministry. A computerized development of a citywide network of evangelism, it is the first of its kind in America. It involves thousands of prayer partners, counselors, and soul-winners—dividing and conquering a city for God. This has quickly become the focal point of the church in that it serves on a very personal level.

In 1982 Jack Wallace was a guest on a Phoenix television program Marja and I were hosting. Jack had heard of me through his brother, who is an addicted street person, and felt I was someone he should meet. He had been told I was a friend of the elite and street (with more emphasis on the latter), and was the kind of person who would give the shirt off his back to the homeless. Jack visited the church and sat in the park section. He saw the vision and heart of this church and, like a powerful line drive directed at him, he "caught" it in the glove of his heart. He continued being challenged by the Word, and recognized again that his calling at the age of eighteen was from God.

Jack went to Bible school and continued his relationships at the church. After a New Year's Eve service we talked in my office into the wee hours of the morning. Jack had been given offers for service, but he felt Phoenix First Assembly was his place. He was willing to be employed outside of the church and volunteer or come inside. Being told there were no funds, he worked at his pool business and contributed like paid staff at every opportunity.

Charley Graves, now one of my EPIC team, heard him preach to the college and career people. He believed Jack should be on staff. Charley offered to pay the bill and Jack came on board. For two years he felt like the church errand boy—but an errand boy for God was a high calling. His old desk and chair were pastor hand-me-downs. He jokes today that maybe part of his anointing came through the woodwork! However, Jack knows better than to accept secondhand revelation!

Jack's high calling and intense love for the ministry provide long hours as the norm. He receives up to eighty phone calls a day—counseling, directing the Watchmen—but as he would say, "No problem!" His dream of a Watchman Ministry grew to include crises lines, overcomers, greeters, singles, visitation, follow-up, AIDS, unwed mothers, in-touch jobs (employment), and housing. His heart expands with every need he confronts. Being involved with care ministries and channeling people with neighborhoods to "keep what we catch" is his daily bread.

Jack Wallace, born to affluency, illustrates homegrown staff—God-given staff pro-vision. He is free to admit, as do others of the eleven who carry the heavy burden, that sometimes the burden is too great, but he thrives on taking God's Word and watching it do an effectual work. At times it is discouraging to pour into people and watch them walk away unchanged. There is a high cost to ministry. Some days he loves it. Some days he hates it and wonders why he was hired. But he has learned from me that he makes a commitment to a church only one year at a time, even though we know, like him, we all are ready to renew that commitment to God. This is God's work and it is marvelous in our eyes.

God takes the common and normal and wants to do great things. God loves to move the ordinary into the extraordinary . . . from His storehouse of pro-vision. Assessments of a person's heart and motives and ministry will ultimately be made in heaven.

The Pastors' School, a part of the life of *everyone* at Phoenix First Assembly, holds a "How We Do It" Monday through Wednesday on the first week of February each year. Started in Davenport with only a handful of pastors, more than three thousand were in attendance in 1989. The school is practical. People come to learn about props for an illustrated sermon, ride one of the fifty buses to the inner city and spend a couple of hours witnessing, then bring the prospects to the evening service—a service that will feature an illustrated sermon— maybe the one where I am literally "raptured" with invisible wires right off the stage. (Seven hundred found Christ when I told of the fate of disbelievers.)

From the Pastors' School on the closing night, thousands move up on Shadow Mountain and stake a new claim for the Lord. The night view from the mountain is inspiring. The lights of Scottsdale and Phoenix reflect from the hills—a magnificent panorama from which to overview commitments made during the past few days. Those claims are later picked up by members who faithfully will pray for those individuals in the coming year. It is another moving night on the mountain. A time for decision and action. A time when ministers and their staff from around the world "renew their strength" (Isa. 41:1).

This chapter opened with two questions: "When is a church big enough?" and "How much staff does it take to meet the pastoral needs of a large church?" If these questions are still unanswered, I and my staff invite you to plan to come to the next Pastors' School. It is guaranteed to be different—and may be a place to offer the pro-vision needed in your location today.

PART FOUR

Super-Vision

13

Contrary to Natural Expectations

WHERE WAS God . . .

. . . When a wheelchair bus had an accident, and two senior citizens were killed?

. . . When a church which desired to do great things for the Lord built a structure for a singing Christmas tree and it collapsed, killing one man and injuring many of the singers?

. . . When tele-evangelists failed and part of the Christian community, by their countenance, portrayed a theology of losers?

Where was God? He was still very much omnipotent and sovereign. We live in a world, even a Christian world, where the perception is that the bigger it is, the better it must be. If it is successful (as some count success), there is a built-in stamp of approval. There is nothing wrong with legitimate growth, but everything wrong with using illegitimate means to further an end.

I believe God is not as excited about superstars as He is about people who are faithful and obedient, who will use their one or multiple talents for the glory of God. This concept is "contrary to natural expectations." When individuals are in trouble or churches are in peril, there appears to be a notion that either God has been caught off-guard, or the situation has not crossed His desk. Faith tends to waver, and a feeling arises that there is little "naturally" that can change the scenario.

This chapter is not about natural options but rather *super*natural means to take the difficulties, impossibilities, and the traumas of life and ministry and turn them around for God's glory. When the apostle Paul wrote the book of Philippians, he was bound with chains. And even more confining—in the restraining manner of the day—he was cuffed to his jailer, an officer of the law! How confining. What a tragedy. But think for a moment of the position of the guard. He was bound to Paul also. That guard had to listen to this preacher throughout his whole shift. In fact four guards per day were assigned to this man of God. During their six-hour shifts, they became "prisoners" of the gospel message that burned in Paul's heart.

I sometimes wonder if those men came on a shift and flipped Roman coins to see who would be the "victim" that night. We see that Paul was not the victim, but the victor. Later in his writings he related that "The seats of Caesar's household salute you" in reference to the converts he had led to Jesus Christ while he was imprisoned. He wrote with great confidence:

> Now I want you to know, brethren, that my circumstances have turned out for the greater progress of the gospel, so that my imprisonment in the cause of Christ, (the things which happened unto me), has become well known throughout the whole praetorian guard and to everyone else. And that most of the brethren, trusting in the Lord because of my imprisonment, have far more courage to speak the word of God without fear. (Phil. 1:12–14 NAS)

He is telling us that his bonds in Christ (the jail experience) are furthering the gospel in the palace and in all the other places.

The word is clear—Paul was leading the guards to Christ. And every new guard gave him a bold opportunity to win a soul, meet the innermost needs of a guard's heart, and heal whatever hurt that man may be carrying. He is also giving us an example—his "bonds" were launching pads to further the kingdom of God. Many of Paul's epistles were written in jail. Some of his greatest writings were written while he was in solitary confinement. We never hear him lamenting his ill fortune. What he is saying in contemporary language is, "I am going to take these handcuffs and club the devil over the head with them right here in jail!"

Paul knew nothing of the victim's role which people today use as a personal handcuff. *He took the crippling handicaps and turned them into challenging inconveniences.*

Remember when the Pharisees and the Sadducees, who were bitter enemies, finally found a common ground in not liking Paul? He was on trial. The Pharisees believed in the resurrection of Christ, the Sadducees did not.

On the stand Paul testified, "I believe in the resurrection."

The Pharisees said, "Amen, brother, we do too."

The Sadducees shouted, "Heresy!" and the two "ecclesiastical" factors started fighting each other. During their heated debate, Paul escaped unnoticed. He was demonstrating this truth: If the devil gives you a stick, use it as a weapon to hit right back!

I have seen a television commercial where an attacker is hitting a person with a big stick, when suddenly the victim takes the stick away from the attacker and goes on the offensive. Can you visualize the picture? If the devil attacks you with his club of lies, defeats, and discouragement, take the club away from this defeated foe and hit him back! We need to assume the victor role. Whatever club the devil uses on you, turn it around and use it against him, contrary to natural expectations!

Paul has given us a supernatural lesson. He wants us to see that we can use everything that happens to us to further the gospel of Jesus Christ. Everything! Note he is not saying everything God allowed to happen to him was for the furtherance of the gospel. He is saying, "I took *everything* that I got and whatever happened to me, and I used it to spread the gospel."

My style as a preacher is to share areas of my personal life. Some say I am too transparent. My desire is to use *everything* as an experiment for the furtherance of the gospel. I want to take that club the devil is using on me, and beat him as hard as I can with his own object of oppression.

When I was young, I was very small for my age. I was timid and felt inferior. I was raised in a less-than-affluent atmosphere in the bottoms of Kansas City, in an area called Armordale, which is in the poorest part of town. That was the location of my dad's church. I often wonder how many are in heaven or will be because my dad, who was very poor when he was a child, shared his personal struggles with them. Dad, because of his background, had a compassionate heart for those in the bonds of poverty. He reached out from his experience, and through his church, to kids with nothing. Dad took the stick of poverty and turned it around and used it against the devil to reclaim people for the kingdom.

Dad's was the first major bus ministry in America. He needed a way to pick those kids up and bring them to church. His own car was already overcrowded. His vision has reached around the country—even to affluent Phoenix.

God took His best gift from heaven, His only Son and forever beat down the devil. "For you know the grace of our Lord Jesus Christ, that though He was rich, yet for your sakes He became poor, that you through His poverty might become rich" (2 Cor. 8:9).

I am confident that had my dad not been a poor child himself, he may not have cared so much about the less fortunate, and may not have made his incredible contribution to winning souls of all ages. Because of his availability to turn things around, bus ministries continue to increase today.

If poverty is your lot, take that "lack" and beat the devil out of Satan with it. Preachers and students are constantly encouraged when I share how average I am, how normal and not very special. I have learned the best way to beat the devil is to realize God can take our nothingness—and when He links it to Almightiness, great things happen. That is contrary to natural expectations!

Taking the stick of poverty, of averageness, of family background and turning it around is the heartbeat of Pastors' School. When we parade our ministries across the platform, I see raised eyebrows and expressions questioning:

Won't that embarrass an unwed mother?
Won't that bag lady feel insecure?
Those educably slow must feel unsafe.
AIDS victims on stage?
Park men, profiles of drugs and alcohol and sin—are they not being exploited?

First, these people are always asked if they want to participate—they are never coerced or under any obligation. It is a personal choice. They make their statement with their willing presence—this is what the devil had done. We have taken that stick from his hand, and turned it into a club against him. Their message reflects lives that are now whole and restored, for the furtherance of the kingdom! Sticks of failure are transformed into lives of wholeness and joy. They join Paul in saying, "The things that happened to me I use for the glory of God."

One of my desires as a pastor is to help each individual realize they have much to offer God. Each has a circumstance that is unique, and each possesses a club to use on the devil.

Paul came from an erudite background. He was from a well-known "upper-crust" tribe. He was a student of the famed Gamaliel, a respected rabbi who lived shortly before the time of Christ. Paul was a member of the Sanhedrin, a distinguished body much like our Senate today. Paul persecuted Christians. He searched them out and dragged them down the street by the hairs on their head. He even marched some to their martyrdom. He writes he was sorry. He was not proud of his early behavior. He was ashamed. Yet he would not become a recluse because the past had no future. He was going to use everything that happened for the furtherance of the gospel.

I have not found anyone who has persecuted or literally dragged Christians down the streets of America. Perhaps that may occur in atheistic countries.

I do not want people to be continually ashamed of what has happened in their lives. "If we confess our sins, He is faithful and just to forgive our sins, and to cleanse us from all unrighteousness" (1 John 1:9). God is in the forgiving business when repentance is sincere. That is why I share both my victories and my failures—sins and things that displease God and are unworthy of Him, as well as projects and plans that didn't happen. I do not share other people's failures. That is not my job. My job is to heal, restore, and deal with other people's sins and failures privately. However, I have learned I can use my own to further the kingdom. I have also learned that we don't keep reminding God of what *He* has forgotten!

My heart is still pierced by a soul-winning failure of mine at my church in Iowa. The relatives of a man ill in the hospital kept asking me to go and see him. The hospital was sixty miles away. This man never came to our church. I made plans to go but something always interfered. I promised myself—soon. The man died. I believe he might have found the Lord if I had gone, since his family said he had respected me. He had made the statement that he would not attend church because he was afraid he would "get saved."

That experience put me into a failure complex. I cried and thought I would die. I asked God over and over to forgive me for being too busy erecting buildings and working to care for the needs of the day. I vowed I would win many to take the place of that dear man.

My mother counseled me with her soft heart, not to share with people that, before my dad died, I had a second-hand experience with Christ. I realize the older I get, that many people have second-hand experiences, and I believe God can use a person even though he or she is seeing God through someone else. I know there are people serving God because their parents or a mentor did. I meet pastors in churches who are serving because their dad did before them, and their experiences mirror their father's. One day, I took the devil's stick of second-hand revelation and beat him with it. My ministry changed!

One of the roughest experiences the devil put on me was when one of our wheelchair buses overturned. It was through no fault of ours, but two precious people died. For consolation I called a clergyman who was one of my mentors. I knew he had gone through a similar experience. I thought he could help me cope, but he was too busy. I am not being critical. He may well have had more pressing issues. He still is one of my heroes. I have learned people cannot always help us when we depend on them. People do not exist just to serve us.

In the midst of the hurt of that wheelchair bus accident, we took the stick the devil used so hard against us and clubbed him again. How? We bought two more buses and increased our ministry.

At Pastors' School a young man became inspired to begin a bus ministry and started with a van. One day he called with broken heart. He said he needed to talk with me about a tragedy. I came on the line and learned that when he had taken the van out to feed ghetto kids, the driver, in backing up, had fatally injured someone. I knew his pain. I had experienced his despair. I could tell him how we took the stick and attacked the devil. He could do it too. He did!

A church "caught" a vision at Pastors' School to produce a singing Christmas tree. The need for a solid foundation built of steel was emphasized. Against that advice, the structure was constructed of wood, and it collapsed at the final performance while the choir was taking a bow.

As a result of that incident more churches have become aware of safety aspects, and are building greater and more secure projects for the glory of God. Contrary to natural expectations, the evil example Satan intended through that tragedy became a triumph for good.

Some are already victorious in life. That is useful to God. It may be wealth or knowledge, a good attitude or health. Use that as a club on the devil.

I have been introduced as the "red-eye bandit." I travel a lot between my services to help other churches and encourage pastors. I always take the last plane out and the first available plane home, so the red eyes are a way of life. The meaning of this introduction I received was I was blessed with health permitting me to fly all night—a positive stick that I beat the devil with often! My stamina is to be used for God.

Visual sight is an asset. But blindness can be turned around. Look at Fanny Crosby. She wrote hundreds of songs for the glory of God. If an individual of God falls or fails, it is a powerful opportunity to turn that failure around and beat the devil with its ramifications.

In 1987 chaos broke loose in this country because there were spiritual failings which appeared to cause any gaining momentum of the church to lose steam and fire. As a result God's people had a tendency to take their eyes off their dreams for revival. Permissiveness and sin had crept into ministries. These events forced the church and its leaders to repent and seek a renewed vision. These incidents granted us an opportunity to remember that crises drive us to our knees to present a humble spirit, in the midst of adversity—whether it is visible leaders or the lesser-known person who falls.

We have been admonished to respect leadership. God directs the body of Christ through ordained and anointed people. Denigrating that responsibility is serious.

David's stance toward Saul's falling offers a biblical formula to follow. David never spoke against Saul, even though Saul had falsely accused him and wanted him killed. In 2 Samuel 1:11–16 we are told that at Saul's death, David "mourned and wept and fasted over the Lord's anointed."

The directly damaging result of these crises events and all-too-common sagas is the sense of betrayal the followers experience. Faithful pastors become suspect. Many facets of the ministry suffer as a by-product.

We know the cross is about forgiveness, but my prayer these days is that even the fallen will allow God to do a work in their hearts, and then take that stick the devil attacked them with and use it as a weapon on that "roaring lion that seeks to destroy." The message I see is that the time has come to *plow up the fallow ground*. Before the glory of God can be fully restored, and the rain of God's righteousness be evidenced, some changes must occur.

This is clearly shown in the autobiographical book of Hosea. He wrote about God's unfailing love in spite of His people's unfaithfulness. He has given the people a message when he said, "Sow with a view to righteousness, reap in accordance with kindness; break up your fallow ground, for it is a time to seek the Lord until He comes to rain righteousness on you" (Hos. 10:12). The implication is strong. The rain of God's righteousness is coming, but in view of the coming rain there is an assignment to God's people to prepare for the rain if the shower's full benefits are to be received. His command is to break up your fallow ground. "Ask rain from the Lord at the time of the spring rain" (Zech. 10:1). God is saying when it is time for the rain to fall, ask for it and He will make "storm clouds and give showers." He wants to send fresh rain on His people.

That rain is already evidenced in great churches. Korea, South America, India, and Africa are some of the countries that have cultivated the land, and where revival rains are falling. The soil must be prepared or the rain will be lost. The soil of our souls needs plowing to produce fruit.

In our lives the ever-present fallow ground needs to be broken up. The power of God must cut through, so as the rain falls, the soil can absorb the moisture. Farmers tell us that it's necessary to go down four to six inches to the hardpan to cultivate the ground before rain will be effective to produce the desired crop. It takes heavy equipment and consistent rototilling to keep the ground receptive to retaining the water. Soil that has grown crops in the past may become dry and unproductive. It becomes hard. Last year's cultivating does not promote this year's harvest. Contrary to natural expectations, a one-time tilling does not do the job. After every rain falls, the fallow ground needs to be broken up all over again. The crustiness, the hardness, and the wild roots must be eliminated.

I believe we need to confront the conditions of our hearts now. Vows made a year ago are not sufficient for today. The Word studied months ago still needs work. Last week's plowing is not enough. We need to recondition the soil of every believer. Abandoned soil produces no fruit. Neglected soil is a wasteland. That is why ministers are out of the ministry today. They did not take the devil's stick and use it to club him with. They fell under his stick on bad soil.

It is fearful to realize that there is soil which cannot receive seed and will not produce a crop. The question is how to break up the ground?

David fasted to break up the ground. Humility gets things from God. John Wesley's revivals were the longest lasting revivals in history. He and his people would fast one and one-half days a week. They learned the skill of breaking up fallow ground.

When the plow goes into a soul, sometimes it is painful and sometimes remorseful. It may be excruciating, for it is said that before God truly makes a person He breaks a person. Humanity's tendency is to call on God *after* failure. God's way is to break up the fallow ground beforehand, and let the rain of His righteousness fall on good, prepared ground. We need to appropriate the value of starting with God in every endeavor. God also wants our spirit to be broken with what breaks His heart. Hearts can be hardened without knowledge. Blind spots keep us from seeing ourselves as we are. David prayed, "Examine me, O Lord, and try me; Test my mind and my heart" (Ps. 26:2 NAS).

Here was a man "after" God's heart—After being a word that means a continual seeking *after* and searching. Jealousy, materialism, and bitterness can invade our hearts. Critical spirits need plowing under. David prayed, "renew a right spirit within me."

Phoenix First Assembly does not have a heart because it feeds the poor and welcomes everyone. It is a church with a heart because it keeps breaking up the fallow ground. I worry about those who get used to the altar calls and those who are anesthetized by my voice and do not hear the Word of the Lord. They become examples of hardened hearts. God does great things when our spirits are open to Him, and He is allowed to plow under what is not worthy. Taking God and His work for granted is a serious offense.

Moses was one of the greats in the Old Testament, but the people got used to him; they even wanted to kill him. God had been doing the miraculous, so the miraculous became common. The outcome? They missed the land that was promised.

During the difficult purging time, the print, television, and broadcast media came to me for interviews. "Crossfire" was here, Ted Koppel's staff called. *Time* magazine wrote an article about us. They all wanted me to make a statement. God said to me, although not audibly, "Go and hide yourself. Spend time with Me." I spent time on the mountain, and my interviews were with Him alone. But in the spring of 1989 the same voice of God said it was time to emerge from the mountain. The ground had been broken up. It was time to speak. It was time to use what was misused, and turn it around for the glory of God. I could no longer dwell on the failings of the past but rise and be strong as He led me, through my commitment to His divine plan.

We need to break up the fallow ground in our lives as we help fallen individuals do the same. Restoration is part of the miracle of Christianity. God promises "a new heart." The time has come to get mean with the devil, never mean with people. I believe the day is here when I want to turn negativeness around. Churches get mad at me for being so positive. The Bible says the "pure in heart see God." I want a pure heart from a broken heart. Even amidst failure all around, I am going to behold the glory of the Lord. I want His "glow-ray" on my life and on this church. A glow-ray that shines across this city and land and into the world, saying we have been with Jesus.

Rain does not fall indiscriminately, but it will fall where churches ask for it and believe they will have it—then reach out to a dying world and see souls saved, the poor lifted and set free. In so doing, we have paralyzed the devil, for we have taken away his wrecking-ball club. *Say a good Amen!*

Turning failure into a fresh focus on the Lord, or hopeless situations into God's glory is contrary to natural expectations. Yet that is the way God operates. His Son was born from the womb of a young woman who was obedient to Him. The forerunner of Jesus and the gospel message, John the Baptist, came through parents who were aged. The Jordan River was overflowing when those children of Israel were to pass toward the Promised Land. God is the architect of impossible situations—contrary to natural expectations.

We expect a fire to burn when dry wood and special kindling are prepared for the match—but not when water and stones have been placed in the fire pan. Yet, contrary to natural expectations, Elijah's twelve barrels of water did not quench the fire God sent.

When we are willing to use the devil's stick against the devil, and to plow up the fallow ground, the results will never be disappointing. Much to the contrary,

> Blessed is the man who trusts in the Lord, and whose trust is the Lord. For he will be like a tree planted by the water, that extends its roots by a stream, and will not fear when the heat comes, but its leaves will be green; and it will not be anxious in a year of drought, neither cease to yield fruit. (Jer. 17:7-8 NAS)

Those operating on the principles, not the options of God, yield fruit in drought and experience the rains of righteousness. No wonder their lives are lived, joyously and reverently, *contrary to natural expectations!*

14

Steps That Stretch the Bounds of Possibility

IN MY MINISTRY I endeavor to stretch the bounds of possibility, and to encourage people with expressions of love and reinforcement. I tell them that if they lose, they lose doing their best. My church is built on more than a dream—it is an attitude based on the belief that with vision, venture, and vigorous effort, a church will grow—any church, not just mine.

In my first church the growth was unprecedented. I left believing God would give me one-hundred-fold (no one is counting!). Any interim or long-term goal setting may have the tendency to fall short of what God will accomplish, yet his planning is precise. Earlier in this book I described my first revival, at the age of sixteen, in Seminole— where I prayed for fifty souls, and fifty responded. Yet the disquieting question was, What if I had asked for one hundred? I believe *we are only as limited as our faith limitations*.

Students of church growth are convinced that the stricter the church obligation, the higher the level of commitment demanded of its members, the more vigorous the growth attained.

The church historian C. Peter Wagner's vision believes the stand of most Pentecostal churches is the reason they thrive. He developed four major criteria:

1. The churches have traditions of purity in their belief in the Bible, Christian doctrine, and life-style. The final authority of Scripture is never in question. They are most often united in primary doctrine. Salvation is paramount. The conversion experience is just that. "Old things are passed away, and all things are become new." Church is the center of family activities and very much part of the life-style of the members.

2. These are churches where prayer is vital. Old traditionalists used to be defined as "Pentecostals that prayed down the power." It was and still is a worthy definition. Prayer is the pillar in church growth.

3. Manifestations of signs and wonders and restoring the reality of hope, healing, and miracles are not new in this denomination. Only of late have other Protestant denominations accepted that the book of Acts is a pattern. Churches have seen an explosive growth of signs and wonders this past decade.

4. Assembly churches have taken seriously God's concern for children and the poor. Many traditional churches have all but abandoned "the least of these." Those who have heeded Jesus' words have experienced the unique blessings of reaching out "to every creature" and have been rewarded.

As a visionary, I work hard to reflect those mandates. I am strict and outspoken in my perception of God's laws. Prayer is the source of my intimacy with God. It is also where I take my disappointments, frustrations, and problems. I can leave the burdens on the mountain that is my place of daily prayer. The Holy Spirit is my prayer partner, and the church is built and kept on that altar of prayer.

I believe in signs and wonders. I believe in political action and take strong stands on issues. However, I am clear that my priority and imperative is to win souls. As for the poor, I am not unlike the majority of preachers in my denomination who were born underprivileged or had fathers who came from poverty. The Assembly church has traditionally been the mainline church of the working class.

I have no intention of moving away from these priorities, even though the denomination in more recent years has been said to be subtly dropping some of those early characteristics. Part of my heart cry is to restore these mandates.

My "Seven Principles" are posted on school kids' bulletin boards and in hundred of pastors' offices. Most have already been a theme throughout this book, but these ultrapractical and spiritual principles deserve listing:

- The vicarious life
- The need makers
- You reap what you sow
- Make every day a masterpiece
- Get better, not bitter
- Live your life in the will of God
- A hand-me-down-God

THE VICARIOUS LIFE

Living the vicarious life means that I attempt to live my life through and for other people. In this manner my goals and dreams are accomplished, be it through my children, my staff, or those in my sphere of influence.

The common denominator in people is that they want to be loved, and they want to be happy. This is not just an American ideal. Cultural anthropologists see these needs throughout the world, although many countries have limited standards with which to measure quality of life. Because being happy and being loved has not proved to be an inalienable right, most individuals are dissatisfied.

Moses, having had a lot of experience with dissatisfied people, wrote, "In the morning you shall say, Would that it were evening! And at evening you shall say, Would that it were morning! because of the dread of your heart which you dread, and for the sight of your eyes which you shall see" (Deut. 28:67).

Probably some of those complaining children of Israel were good at wishing the days were not so long on their journeyings. With their track record they were a long time in the wilderness. It appeared the trip would never end.

Unhappy people are in world-class proportions. As a pastor it would be easy to spend most of the time counseling the troubled. The reason is the same today as it was when Moses was moving them along—

people have their eyes on themselves. The most unhappy and unloved individuals are those who look *within* instead of turning their attention and their affections and desires *without* on others.

Part of the problem is what I call the "Yesterday and Tomorrow Syndrome." It starts when a small child watches his older sibling go to school and says, "I can't wait to go to school." In kindergarten at last he "can't wait" for first grade—junior high—high school and then college. In the interim the kid wishes for success on teams, with friends—and the merry-go-round goes round and round. It is like a greyhound chasing a rabbit—he never catches it.

Symbolic of our society is a *Reader's Digest* story of a pilot who used to fly out of his way on his commercial course to tip his wings to a favorite location. The place was a small creek where the pilot used to fish as a boy. He admitted to days when he would see a plane fly overhead, and dream he was flying that plane. Now that he was an adult, he wished he was back fishing on the banks of that creek—an illustration of yesterday and tomorrow and the striving and unhappiness in between.

From school, young people date and get married. A child comes and the circle of life keeps going on, with dreams now shattered and desires unfulfilled. Mothers wish their offspring would grow up. When they are grown, they wish for the days when they were toddlers. The problem is that we do not have enough sense to be happy today while yesterday was today. I am convinced the best age is the age that I am at this moment. "This is the day which the Lord has made; let us rejoice and be glad in it" (Ps. 118:24). Today is a day of opportunity. Today is a day of blessing. We all have a tendency to wish for another time. But I am turned on about today. "Now is the accepted time. Now is the day of salvation!"

We are told that more people will live in the twentieth century than all the previous nineteen centuries combined. We have the means to reach these people as never before in history. I have no time to live in the past, nor a lot of time to wait for tomorrow. *I want to savor today*—to look at today the way I looked at tomorrow yesterday—and to look at today the way that you will look at yesterday tomorrow! Yesterday we thought that tomorrow was a wonderful day. Now tomorrow is here. So have a wonderful day!

I want to encourage you to not just savor today, but to enjoy the trip as much as you enjoy the destination. A great man said that preparation for revival is revival. It has been an honor many times to receive the growth awards for our church. The joy for me comes not in the awards, but the fun and work and sharing that took us there.

Some people talk about when they get to heaven, it will be great . . . and it will. But remember the Bible says, "Thy kingdom come, Thy will be done, on *earth* as it is in heaven." Let me encourage you to find happiness within your possibilities. Everyone has the capacity of stretching their possibilities. If your community is small, take it big for God. For He is all and in all. If you are confined to a wheelchair, stretch your influence in that nursing home. Let your witness for God reach not just to a roommate, but a nurse's aid or delivery boy. Take it all and then some!

Find happiness in your means. I went from a jeep to a 1949 powder-blue Plymouth. Then I saved and got a peach and white Plymouth. I have run the gamut on cars. Cars are not happiness. Joy comes from living within your means, and still doing great things for God and those dear to you.

Do not predict tomorrow. I used to ask for 10 percent of the city where I pastored. At the same time I wondered what would happen if the church had to go underground. Giving *today* my all will help me cross that future dateline when it arrives.

Never want to leave where you are. The grass that is greener on the other side too often proves to be artificial turf. Believe that the grass is greenest on your side. You have the best family, the best church, and the best God! Pulpits change hands at a high frequency because pastors jump at the thought of "better opportunities." I have made a life commitment to my people that only God can break.

When you live in Christ for today, there is inexpressible joy. Part of it stems from the other todays, when you invested your life in another, and that one now reports he is reinvesting in another. This is the vicarious life, and the chain reaction goes on. Living your life through others and for others has to be one of the Christian's true secrets of success.

THE NEED MAKERS

Some of the wonderful Spanish ladies in our church heard that I loved good tamales. On occasion these ladies will leave a pan of fresh tamales at my office. There will be a note expressing their love. These dear women are fulfilling a need for me—they are showing their love. I also believe it fulfills a need of theirs, for we all need to be needed. Hattie, who contends you have to be black to make ribs, brings me ribs each month. They are *the* best!

Just before Pastor's Conference one year, Jack Wallace of my staff and Craig Smith, whose story you read in this book, decided to encourage their pastor! Both were concerned that I was carrying a very heavy load, and several thousand incoming pastors was a great responsibility. These men know my heart, and have seen my desire that people catch the vision of living their lives vicariously for others and for God. They determined to prepare me for my task.

Shortly before the first meeting, I slipped into my office. I stopped, wondering if it was really my office. From the ceiling notes were suspended on computer paper—notes saying that I would be anointed for that service, that I would bless those pastors, and I should feel encouraged. On my desk was a series of dinner plates with unusual fare created for "their pastor." By each plate there was a knife and fork. One plate held ten-penny nails. The note attached said, "Men like Tommy Barnett do not eat regular breakfasts, they eat nails. They are tough!" Next there was a box of Wheaties with Michael Jordan's picture cut out and mine inserted. The message was clear! The next plate held a can of power-steering fluid, except the "steering" had been deleted and the tag now read, "Normal men drink orange juice for breakfast, but men like Tommy Barnett drink *power* fluid!" In the bathroom was a heavy steel brush. The note attached stated, "Normal men comb their hair with plastic combs. Tommy Barnett needs a steel brush for his massive mane!" (The brush almost annihilated my scalp!) The last item was an axe. The message, "Men like Tommy Barnett do not use razors to shave, they use axes!"

Some might say, "For what purpose that waste?" I want you to know those men were used to bring me a great big smile. Also I was given an opening illustration for my Pastors' School. We all had fun. I needed my friends Craig and Jack, and they needed me. All of my staff excel in keeping me encouraged.

What I later learned, after Pastors' School was over, and God had blessed us with results, those two men had spent much time praying over my chair and office that the anointing would indeed come, and that God would shower His blessing.

People are attracted because they are needed. They stay because they become essential in the plan of God for taking our city. Anybody and everybody can make somebody happy and show God's love. Isn't that what people are looking for?

I encourage my congregation to go out and find a need and become one of the need makers. It is amazing what they come up with, and what they are willing to do—everything from political action to caring for the baptismal room. In the Appendix you will find some of the needs people are fulfilling. By the time this comes off the press, the list will have increased. That's what happens when you have a church willing to make needs their priority.

Needs at Christmas are vast. All of our children receive gifts. For many of the bus children ours will be the only gifts that they receive. We give away more than five thousand presents. It is a Christmas gift just to see those kids come down the aisle to get their presents. The singing Christmas tree is lit and is the largest tree they have ever seen. The lights on the tree and the tears in the eyes of the choir members, who form the tree ornaments, reflect the sparkle in their eyes. The carols are sung and the two mountains of presents—one for boys and one for girls—are heaped with wonderfully wrapped parcels.

One little child who had never seen such extravagance before turned to his bus pastor and inquired, "Is this heaven?" A little boy had prayed for an electric train. At a suggested five dollar per gift limit a train was unlikely, and the odds against it being in the mountain of boys' toys were not good. When the boy was given his gift, God knew he needed an answered prayer. Scores of bicycles and other expensive items are given each year, but that little lad got the electric train from the jumble of joy under the tree.

One of my good memories was the year we also prepared five thousand gifts for Rosie Grier's ministry in Los Angeles. We put them on a bus and gave him the bus, too! That was such a blessing!

Napoleon Hill said that the way to get rich was to find the world's greatest need and supply it. We already know that need. People will be happy and be loved only if they know the love of the Lord Jesus, and then start giving that love away. That *is* happiness.

YOU REAP WHAT YOU SOW

Every day when I wake up, it is like Christmas in my heart. I am eager for another day with the Lord. Headed toward the mountain with my big container of coffee, I *anticipate* what God will do in my life and in my church. If the day includes going to the ball games of my boys, I will be the loudest to cheer them on and boo the umpires. No matter the schedule, I will find time to appreciate my family. If a staff meeting is called, I will thank God in advance for those men who are my co-laborers with God—the best people in the world. My heart will expand again with gratitude and thankfulness for the Lord Jesus Christ and the person of the Holy Spirit.

Does that sound a bit maudlin? Or effusively sentimental? Believe me, it is true! For I believe in all areas of life *you reap what you sow.*

God has entrusted me with only one life. At fifty-two years old, I cannot waste a moment. It is such a privilege to be on God's team. I still have dreams and plans for tomorrow, but *today* is my focus. I never want to be in the position of looking back and pondering, "What if?" Now is what matters.

Scores of people live in those two words when they retire. "What if?" Kids that are defeated in sports say, "What if?" Donny Moore, a former pitcher for the California Angels, took his life in 1989 because of missing a crucial pitch in a playoff game a couple of years previously. There were too many "What if's?" I will always apply myself more and keep trying harder, for I never want to be a victim of the "if's."

I see people who have little means accomplish monumental exploits for God. I study those with abundance, and wonder if the day will come when they ask, "What if?" We have been promised that the "joy of the Lord is our strength." That no matter the economic structure, "fullness of joy" comes from the true source—the holy men of God: Father, Son, and Holy Spirit.

I believe as I prepare my heart each day to "sow" seeds of the Spirit's fruit, I will reap lavish benefits. Sir Laurence Olivier had a great, tragic line: "If I had everything I would have everything."

There are no conditions on God's Word as He promises us "joy unspeakable and full of glory." If you sow it, I guarantee you will reap it. In everything!

Whatsoever a man sows, that he will also reap, For he who sows to his flesh will of the flesh reap corruption, but he who sows to the Spirit will reap everlasting life. And let us not grow weary in well doing, for in due season we shall reap if we faint not. (Gal. 6:7–9)

What you want to reap tomorrow, you plant today. What you want to find for yourself, you start by giving it away. If you need to be inspired, start inspiring someone else.

Often when I prepare to preach or when I am in the pulpit or speaking at a church or great convention, I will say to myself, *Who needs to hear these words the most?* The answer usually comes back, *I do!*

People want two things, love and happiness. Sow it and you will reap it! And the best place to do that is to find a person who needs our Lord. Sow seeds of Christ's love and joy and watch out! The love and joy, like a precise boomerang, will come right back to you. And you will have another person to take with you to glory.

Sowing and reaping have an ugly flip side. If you sow dissension, judgmentalism, fault-finding, and disbelief, you reap the same. Harsh as it may sound, Jesus spoke to the issue, "Judge not lest you be judged."

Brag on those who are dear to you and those who are not! Encourage your leaders and give "good press" to your enemies. In the Sermon on the Mount, Jesus painted a lovely portrait of the blessed! And the outcome of blessing: "Rejoice and be exceedingly glad, for great is your reward in heaven" (Matt. 5:12).

MAKE EVERY DAY A MASTERPIECE

Life can be made to resemble a magnificent, homemade quilt. Part of the coloring is brilliant and daring, another part is soft and provides background. During the years when the quilt is being put together, an onlooker may see only the underneath. Hanging from the underside are threads and tied knots. Pieces of material may hang unfinished; yarn and embroidery threads may be matted and in disarray. Yet little by little, the quilt is put together in the hands of its creator. The process may be slow, but the beauty is developing along the way.

An old, old story is told of a grandchild visiting her grandma. Grandma was making one more of her famous quilts for this last grandchild. When the ten year old viewed the quilt, she was disappointed. "Grandma, it looks awful. It isn't like the one you made for my big sister."

Grandma quietly lifted the quilt and turned it over. The child had been looking at the wrong side.

This resembles people. From the underside of heaven there are times when the tied knots are in our stomachs, when the hanging threads feel so taut they could break, when the colors are drained, and the background gray with a grim forecast. That is the time to remember that we, as God's creation, are "fearfully and wonderfully made," and as His creation we are destined for the throne. From His side, in the Ephesians concept, we are becoming what we already are *"in Christ."* Complete. Finished. Perfect!

In an informal survey of ministers and staff people of all denominations, the highest percentage had some form of *leaving* on their minds. The fabric of their lives and church was not coordinated, and a love affair with their congregations was seldom in evidence. I would like to wrap my arms around these leaders, and tell them to start making every day a masterpiece until the Master Designer moves you on. Never be controlled by outward circumstance, but by inward sources.

General MacArthur, in a taped interview, said he could tell when people were getting older—they enjoyed the sunset more than the sunrise. I do not like to disagree with the old patriot, but I prefer the sunrises, and always will! Each one formed by my Father-God introduces the dawn of a new day, with a fresh opportunity to present to Him another masterpiece.

GET BETTER, NOT BITTER

I think of Elaine, in my church, spending the major portion of her life in a wheelchair. She says she has spent many, many days alone, but never a lonely day—since Jesus became her Savior.

With a scarred face and back a teenaged boy, product of inner-city abuse and a stepfather's hatred, stood in our parking lot and shared how the bus ministry brought hope to his damaged world. He bears the scars of the past but is in night school, working a day shift in two fast-food restaurants so he can be all God wants him to be. His love for this ministry carries with it a determination to prepare himself to pick up other little ghetto kids and bring them hope and love. Bitter? He has every reason to be. But through people's care for the lost and needy, he discovered a better way. He says, "I am striving for a more excellent way. I can't spell excellent yet, but before long I will. However, I can practice excellence in everything I do. Pastor says the past has no future. I'm making my life a masterpiece of *better*ness, not bitterness. Praise God!"

Paul had many bitter experiences that proved better. He dreamed of preaching in Spain, and his dream brought him to a Roman prison cell. Like all of us, Paul never met Jesus in person, but his faith was so solid that he withstood torture and prison for the gospel.

Part of Paul's secret was his Selah time. Here was a brilliant man who never could have enough of the Word as he knew it. He diligently studied, even in prison. The apostle was aging and near death, the result of persecution under Nero. Alone and cold in his cell, he wrote to his son in the faith: "When you come bring the cloak which I left at Troas with Carpus, and the books, especially the parchments" (2 Tim. 4:13 NAS). The old prophet wanted to study. The coat he needed for warmth. The books were papyrus rolls and the parchments—skins of vellum used for precious documents, his copies of portions of the Old Testament. What an example of making the bitter better!

When I was about five years old, I had an opportunity to get a bitter spirit about deacons. They did not always support my dad. I would hear Dad and Mother talk about some of the events in the church that were alarming. I clearly recall a day when Dad, with my mother supporting him, came home from church sobbing. Work had not gone well. I was sad and mad. I might have been a little guy, but I had great pride in my dad. I picked up my lasso and my roping sticks and was headed for the church to help God discipline those deacons who had made my daddy cry. But Dad grabbed my arm.

He stopped me and told me some people in the church were hard to get along with, but most of the people of God were good people—the best people in the world. I could have bitterly held that childish memory in my heart and had it poison my relationships with deacons, but Dad squelched it right there. Some gifts are meant to last for generations. His gift to me of forgiving people and loving them—always—is being passed on to my children, and God willing, will be passed to theirs!

On another occasion the deacons came to my rescue. It was Halloween, and while we went to church, I left a candle burning in my jack-o-lantern, which was on the chest of drawers. During the service we heard the fire engines, and we saw the parsonage in flames. I knew who had caused that fire. The incriminating evidence was overwhelming—the burned chest of drawers and the remains of my pumpkin.

That deacon board supported me and talked about faulty wiring that they needed to replace. They could have been malicious and vindictive. They could have humiliated the pastor's only child. But God's people are good people! I have always chosen to remember that the deacons protected me rather than that they were hurtful to my dad—the better versus the bitter. I have loved my deacon boards to this day, although there are times, to be honest, when some have stretched those bounds of possibility!

LIVE YOUR LIFE IN THE WILL OF GOD

How do you know God's will and what the difference is between a call and a burden are questions that come frequently across my desk.

I believe God wants us to live in His will. It is not such a complicated place. There is no advantage to God eclipsing His will from our view. Much is already revealed.

It is well known that God is not willing that any should perish. If a person is born again, he has started heeding the Word of God by taking Him at His Word, and receiving eternal life. We are told to take the good news to those who know not the Lord and His saving grace. If people share their faith, they are doing the *will* of God.

There is no mystery surrounding the words of Micah, in the Old Testament. "He has shown you, O man, what is good; and what does the Lord require of you but to do justly, and to love mercy, and to walk humbly with your God?" (Micah 6:8).

When we take the knowledge we have and appropriate it, we are living in the will of God.

I have heard kids in Bible college say they likened the will of God to enlisting in the service. They would never know where they might be placed. I tell them that the will of God never leads us where the grace of God does not precede. We were won to the Lord by love, not by force—and that same love leads.

I have shared that God specifically *called* me into the ministry. His call was not of my doing. I accepted that call. I knew it was the sovereign will of God for me. I also have experienced that the call of God comes before the burdens He places on our hearts.

The Bible tells us in Acts 8 of a revival meeting that Philip was preaching in Samaria. People were getting saved. There were so many converts, the apostles had sent Peter and John to help with the new believers. Right in the midst of the evangelistic campaign, Philip got a call from God to go to the desert of Gaza. The Gaza Strip provided no density of population. Philip had no burden for the area, but he responded to God's call by going, and *after* he arrived, found the Ethiopian eunuch reading Scripture and led him to understanding.

I look for danger signals when I hear people say they are responding to a burden. Burdens have a way of changing shoulders. A call of God is without repentance. Living in the will of God means living for Him today, doing what is revealed and trusting Him to reveal the rest. He will! I know because when I was a young evangelist, I used to get a burden for every place I preached in. I got stirred. I loved the people. I saw opportunity. I knew that was the place for me. It happened in Beirut, London, India, the Philippines, and a lot of American cities. God's call took me to none of those places to serve Him in a church. His will turned out to be locations I had no burden for: Davenport and Phoenix. It was after I answered His call that I had the burden, and now I rest in the full knowledge that I am living my life in the will of God.

A HAND-ME-DOWN GOD

People in our Saturday Soul-Winning Society get excited about the fruit of their labor. There is no greater thrill than that of bringing a person to Jesus. However, for the person, the greater thrill will come when they experience the Lord firsthand—not through the one who brings them or even teaches them, but for themselves.

A clear illustration is the story of the woman at the well. Jesus, who made us, is intimately associated with every area of our lives. He knew this woman of Samaria well. The story relates that when Jesus needed to go through Samaria, He already knew her need right along with her shortcomings and jaded history before He first encountered her. She offered Him a drink of water. He responded, "If you knew the gift of God, and who it is who says to you, Give me a drink, you would have asked Him, and He would have given you living water" (John 4:10 NAS). Jesus *knew* her problem was not just the many husbands and relationships—those were symptoms of her unrecognized desire for an eternal relationship that only God can give. She took the living water, and became an instant minister of the good news.

"Come and see the Man," she would tell her friends. They knew she had been with many men, but this was different. She was different. They came and believed. How? "By the word of the woman." Through this woman and all soul-winners, people see God through others' eyes and by the power of His Spirit. The story does not end there. John's account says, "Many more believed because of *His* own word." It is shown that they believed the woman, but it was confirmed through a firsthand experience with Jesus. "Then they said to the woman, Now we believe because we have heard Him ourselves, not just because of what you told us. He is indeed the Savior of the world" (John 4:42).

As we point people to Christ, it is essential that they see Him face to face, and that we all spend that time with Him so people will know that we have been with the Lord.

I never deny there is power in secondhand revelation. I lived it and know it is true. However, when we come to a place of seeking nothing second best, that is the place where everything about Him comes together, and "we *know* what we know firsthand."

Job understood when he wrote, " 'I have heard of You by the hearing of the ear, but now my eye sees You' " (Job 42:5). It was one experience to read about or hear about God—quite a different one to truly experience Him personally.

These seven principles have helped form my walk with God. They may be oversimplified, but they work.

I would like to be known as a champion of winning souls and preaching the Word of God. I want Him on the highways and off-ramps of my life—guiding, directing, correcting, and encouraging.

How I love it when He stretches me and reshapes me and fills me with Himself. I do my best to live a vicarious life. I will never give up searching for needs to fill and giving away what I need. Each day is designed in my heart to become a masterpiece. Therefore I cannot get bitter, not when I am seeking to walk in His will, and my revelations come directly from Him. I would encourage each reader to do the same. With Christ all things are possible.

15

The Super-Vision of the Holy Spirit

ONE OF the most magnificent days in my life was the day I realized that the Holy Spirit is not an experience but a person! He is not abstract dogma or mysticism. The Holy Spirit is not enthusiasm and excitement. He is indeed a person! The late A. W. Tozer wrote:

The Holy Spirit is a Person. Put that down in capital letters—that the Holy Spirit is not only a Being having another mode of existence, but He is Himself a Person, with all the qualities and powers of personality. He is not matter, but He is substance. The Holy Spirit is often thought of as a beneficent wind that blows across the Church. If you think of the Holy Spirit as being literally a wind, a breath, then you think of Him as nonpersonal and nonindividual. But the Holy Spirit has will and intelligence and feeling and knowledge and sympathy and ability to love and see and think and hear and speak and desire the same as any person has. (A. W. Tozer, *How to Be Filled with the Holy Spirit*)

That day the Holy Spirit became my head pastor, teacher, and my prayer partner. I experienced a revolution in my Christian life as He, like a fresh breeze, revealed Himself to me. Refreshing! Infectious! Intimately personal!

I understood that the Holy Spirit wanted to be viable in my life. I knew that I yearned for His fullness. I had a hunger and thirst for firsthand satisfaction. I possessed a *willingness to match His eagerness.* He began a renovation process on my whole inner life.

During a question-and-answer session several years ago at a men's breakfast, someone asked why I did not speak more on the Holy Spirit. I was somewhat taken aback. I knew in my heart that I mentioned the Holy Spirit often as an *experience,* and people in our church were filled with the Holy Spirit.

Today that question is not an issue, for when I moved from an experience to an intensely personal relationship, things were different. I believe that outside of salvation, and right alongside of prayer, one of the greatest truths I learned was that of the Holy Spirit being a person.

One of the signs pointing to an eleventh hour for the church is the great wave of the Holy Spirit that is sweeping the world. All indications, in my opinion, point to the Lord's imminent return.

As a teenager in 1954, I began to preach. In 1970 I pastored my first church. In 1979 I came to Phoenix. I have never wanted for a place to preach—a blessing that comes from God alone, but there have been heavy struggles in my walk with God. I knew about the Holy Spirit theologically, and I knew about the Holy Spirit legalistically. But personally we were not close. I was born again. I was indwelt by the Spirit. I had received the baptism of the Holy Spirit, but I did not *know* the Holy Spirit. It was one thing to know about Him, and another to know Him well. One day God gave me new enlightenment on the subject of the Comforter or Lawyer:

> If ye love Me, keep my commandments. And I will pray the Father, and He shall give you another Comforter, that he may abide with you forever: Even the Spirit of truth; whom the world cannot receive, because it seeth him not, neither knoweth him: but ye know him; for he dwelleth with you, and shall be in you. (John 14:15–18)

When I met Him as a person, the One called to be beside me and to help me, great power flowed into my life—for with the Holy Spirit, nothing is impossible.

The majority of church members have not heard the message of the Holy Spirit's being a person. He is not a thing. He is a distinct individual. He has personality. He has wisdom. He is full of knowledge and emotion, and He has volition. I also learned that He was not only a distinct personality, but a delicate one. If He is ignored, He is grieved, and His ever-available resource is quenched.

He was given to become part of the family of God, the Trinity. If family members are ignored or not acknowledged, they become unhappy. If I stayed home all day and never talked with my wife or my children, they would be unhappy. Similarly the Holy Spirit wants to be included.

As Jesus was about to leave the earth, He gathered His disciples around Him, and announced He was going to leave them and return to His Father in heaven. This gathering played havoc with their hearts, because these were men who had left their homes, their families, and their businesses to follow Him. The proclamation was met with mixed emotion. They became depressed. They felt violated. They were at a loss and literally unsettled. Jesus always had a way of quieting the fear of His followers. This meeting was no exception. His message to them was to not be worried, because He was praying to the Father to send another Comforter to always be present with them.

To replace Him was an awesome task, so the Father sent the Holy Spirit—an awesome person. This replacement had the qualities that Jesus possessed, for heaven never sends second best! Jesus said it was better for Him to leave because only then can the Comforter come and dwell within. It is an amazing revelation that Jesus had already accomplished what He had come for: to fight against sin, sickness, and the devil. He conquered them all at the cross. Now the Holy Spirit had come to dispense all the potential blessings reserved for those who would receive Him.

The Holy Spirit was in a better position than Jesus Christ was to fill that empty place of God in us. If Jesus healed, so could He. When Jesus comforted, so would He. Both could perform miracles. They were totally and equally endowed by the Father. But as Jesus' life went to the Father, the Holy Spirit descended into the hearts of believers. No longer would there be a sense of aloneness.

Now the Holy Spirit did not come in a human body like Jesus. The Bible says He came as the wind. That is easy to understand, because the wind is always with us. The wind cannot be seen, but it can be felt. Even when it isn't apparent, it is always present, silently doing the job.

Even so the Holy Spirit is ever present, pointing people to Jesus, exalting the Father—recognized by an act of our willingness to acknowledge His presence.

When I was baptized in the Holy Spirit, I knew His power. I knew He was the force from God. But I still did not know Him as a person; therefore for all those years I grieved Him. God must be revered, His Son glorified, and the Holy Spirit recognized. I never again want to be guilty of neglecting the Holy Spirit. He will never be abandoned in my life. I welcome Him often throughout the day.

It was a blessing when I accepted the Holy Spirit as my prayer partner. I now run my petitions to the Father by the Holy Spirit before I present them through Jesus. I may say to Him that I need a new coat, and since I sometimes preach in cold climates, it would be nice to have a designer coat with a mink collar. Often He convinces me that while He understands a coat is needed, the designer label and fur collar are not necessary for warmth, so I present my prayer to the Father through Jesus and am blessed with a generic coat.

If that sounds simplistic, I'd like you to consider the childlikeness Jesus suggested we follow when we pray. I believe the Holy Spirit filters out the extraneous in my prayer life, and my answers are expedited. In past generations it was thought praying to the Holy Spirit was considered heresy. Jesus is our intercessor and the Holy Spirit works on our behalf—toward those whose hearts are toward Him.

I also talk with Him often during the day. There is no use being silent when I am on an airplane or driving alone in a car. He is with me; therefore, I have learned the joy of acknowledging this incredible person. As I ask Him to bring circumstances, people, the best routes to travel, I have answers as specific as the person who has listened and acted on my behalf.

I am convinced that the single most effective reason for our church growth is the Holy Spirit. I do what I can do, and *the Holy Spirit does what I cannot do.* If my churches are measured by what I can do, that is "natural" effort. Great things happen only "supernaturally." "And they were utterly astonished, saying He has done all things well; He makes even the deaf to hear, and the dumb to speak" (Mark 7:37). Even Jesus, who is our example, was filled with the Holy Spirit. John 3:34 recounts Jesus being filled with the Spirit "without measure."

And Ephesians 5:18 assures us that we too may be "filled with the Spirit."

It is well known that the Holy Spirit comes to live in the Christian upon salvation. When Jesus Christ comes into a heart, the Holy Spirit comes with Him, for the Bible says no one can be saved unless the Holy Spirit draws them. The Bible tells us that through the filling of the Holy Spirit, the gifts of the Spirit are activated, and the evidences are manifest.

The anointing of the Holy Spirit is a proven truth that has touched my life on three occasions, and there may be more in the future. From the Old Testament we know that David was anointed three times during his life: once in a field to be king, once over a portion of Judea, and the last time over all of Israel. I believe God anoints us for His purpose.

My first anointing was in that little town of Seminole, Texas. Before that first meeting I was scared to death. I will never forget that day when I was almost ready to preach and I prayed, "Oh, God, I don't want to just preach because my daddy or grandaddy did. I want it to be You, God." And I felt something indiscernible pour into my body. My first anointing.

The second time was in Davenport. Again I was a scared little preacher, newly moved into a paint-peeling office. I was so insecure that I didn't think even the seventy-six who had come that day would stick with me for long. During those early days I was so worried about my congregation that if I realized someone was absent, I would leave during the song service, return to my little office, and call that home. If they answered, I hung up, encouraged that they were at least at home and not at another church. It was at that first service that I again asked God to anoint me. He did not forget me, and the outpouring warmed my being with His answer to my desperate prayer.

The third time came on the day we were to dedicate our new church building, which seats seven thousand. That opening service I came to the door and looked out over the vast expanse, jammed with people. It was more than filled—people were packed in the aisles. My response? I literally wanted to run as fast as I could to the farthest destination. I was pragmatic enough to return to my office, still unsure that I wouldn't jump into my car and just keep driving. I fell on my old chair and prayed, "God, this is a big church, and they've got a little preacher. I am not qualified to preach in this building. God, You have to help me. I lack natural ability. I am qualified *only* in the supernatural. I need the "super-vision" of your Spirit."

Suddenly it was like a light shining, penetrating my soul. I don't know how it happened. I just know that it was like God's great rays of glory pouring in and I felt strength and boldness. I knew thousands of men were more capable, but for some reason, I had been chosen.

I left that office refreshed, and walked on that platform and preached on Jesus, the altogether lovely One. I knew He had prepared me. My expectation was of God. *I knew that He had expectations of me.* I am, through the Holy Spirit, to become His fruitful vine. The older I get, the more I believe that reasonable service is service that does not always come from intellect, approval, or stature. *I bring Him glory only as I bear fruit.* I must continue to break up the fallow ground, for "He who tills his land will have plenty of fruit, but he who follows empty pursuits will have poverty in plenty" (Prov. 28:19).

If there was advice, a message, or a burning desire that I would want to give to everyone it would be to meet the Holy Spirit as a person. Too much of evangelism, vision, and planning in the church today is in the power of a man. God directs His work by the operation of the Holy Spirit. Too many accept a substandard New Testament pattern. The social overtakes the spiritual. Our models become successful business-people, celebrated athletes, and exciting personalities. That may be natural. The supernatural Christian life is not static. It is dynamic, ex-panding, and deepening.

Paul wrote an incredible truth on the Holy Spirit to Timothy: "For I know whom I have believed and I am convinced that *He is able to guard* what I have entrusted to Him until that day" (2 Tim. 1:12, emphasis added). We know when that we come to Jesus Christ and His Spirit indwells, He does take our lives and "guards" them. The truth does not stop there. In verse 14 Paul reverses the procedure! "Guard through the Holy Spirit who dwells in us, the treasure which has been entrusted to you."

What treasure has the person of the Holy Spirit entrusted to us? Here are three valued truths.

• *First He entrusted us with His glory!* Hours before Jesus went to the cross He shared why He came to earth, and why He would die. "I have glorified my Father." Now He is saying go and do likewise. The treasure entrusted to us is His glory. What does it mean to glorify God? Luke 5 tells us to glorify Him for what He has done for us; Romans 1 to honor Him for who He is. Revelations 4 reminds us He is worthy. His shekinah glory was seen in Exodus in the tabernacle. It filled the place. That glory was a glory that shone so as to reflect and reveal the character of God.

What a liberating truth for those who ask, "What can I do for God?" It is simple. Glorify Him in word and deed. Through the Holy Spirit that is within you, reveal and reflect the character of God. People will see that kind of glory.

* *The second thing entrusted to us is the ministry of reconciliation.*

Now all these things are from God, who reconciled us to Himself through Christ, and gave us the ministry of reconciliation, Namely that God was in Christ reconciling the world to Himself, not counting their trespasses against them, and He has committed to us the word of reconciliation. (2 Cor. 5:18, 19)

How do we minister that truth? Again, "through the Holy Spirit that is within us."

* *The third is the necessity to teach, as found in 2 Timothy 2:2.* "And the things which you have heard from Me in the presence of many witnesses, these entrust to many faithful men, who will be able to teach others also." How do we learn to teach? Through the Holy Spirit within us . . . that great resident Truth Teacher! Someone has said it is like having God in our pocket!

We are admonished to teach our children, to share the things we have learned with a neighbor or friend or associate. Keep spreading the Word, and those you teach will teach others and others. Christianity then will become self-propagating. The person of the Holy Spirit longs to lead you into new dimensions, if you have entrusted your life to Him.

God's divine plan of redemption was proposed by Him. His only son Jesus secured the plan, and granted us the Holy Spirit in person to apply the truth to our lives.

My desire is that His holy presence will so fill your life with His invisible means of support, that you will venture forth to accomplish unprecedented exploits for Him—limited only by His limitless resource.

> Holy Spirit, all divine,
> Dwell within this heart of mine;
> Cast out every idol throne,
> Reign supreme—and reign alone.
> —Andrew Reed
> "Holy Ghost, with Light Divine"

16

Portraits of Vision: An Epilogue

IF PASTOR Barnett's years of ministry were to be translated into portraits of his uncompromising vision, they could be hung in a magnificent gallery. Over the entry doors of this imaginary memory lane would be a bold, textured banner heralding:

FOR THE GLORY OF THE LORD!

The inside walls would be covered with transparencies and photographs, sketches, and watercolors of memories of the faithfulness of God through the years.

To the right would be pictures of bus kids with balloons and Bibles, hot dogs, and Christmas presents—all brightly lit in the colors of love and commitment. Prominent in the foreground would be photographs of the scores of individuals who have kept those buses running: mechanics, drivers, bus pastors, assistants, and parents.

Past that "showing" is the handicapped section. Some of these dear people were formerly framed in tragedy, but through the love of God's people, they have been retouched in triumph.

Wide-angle lenses were needed to capture massive crowds of the past. For example, there is the square in Manila, and the sinkhole of human suffering called Calcutta, where the etchings show pain and struggle and undernourishment . . . the only hope being heaven.

Another portrait in this memory lane is of an old man. His face is scarred, and the artist used harsh colors and textures to display his anxiety and the toll of addictions. One step to the right is another portrait—resembling the same old man, but with a new countenance, his eyes focused on a Bible. The caption on these classic before-and-after pictures reads, "If any man be in Christ, he is a new creation." This man represents street and park people, and the homeless scenes that are very evidenced within these walls.

Strong, steel frames hold pictures of athletes. Some are captured on an inner-city playground. Various renderings of these champions are a source of delight to the fans. Here is a designated section to recall the famous plays of the well known, and to remember that their love of God supersedes even their sports skill. Glass cases display baseballs signed by Hall of Fame members, and footballs with the unique signatures of Heisman trophy recipients now serving God. A weathered painting on real-life canvas is of Pastor Barnett's favorite basketball goal. The background is the park, and his sons comprise his "first-string team."

Soft pastels and colors represent the women of the past who have served and fixed suppers, helped brides, consoled the grieving, and always been graciously available. Food banks and clothes closets for the less fortunate are painted in consistency and dependability, then encased in faithfulness.

The next section holds museum quality pieces. Like a prism reflecting a rainbow of sound, musicians who fill everybody's life are pictured in celebrations of praise. Choral groups and orchestras, in rich baritone colors, catch high soprano hues. These tapestries of music resonate inside and outside the gallery.

Colors of the Fourth of July are bold. Impressions of fireworks flash in the air. Memories of altar calls bring meaning to this slide presentation, which includes a singing Christmas tree and a living Lord's Last Supper. Past performances have blessed spectators in Kansas City, Davenport, and Phoenix.

The global section features missions. Thatched roofs fascinate the children. Dense, black brushings magnify the places where people have never heard of Jesus. There is still so much light needed to dispel the darkness of those multitudes who never have heard of Jesus.

What a contrast follows. Splashes of joy with great intensity. Modern, impressionistic, and free-form are the portraits of the Watchmen who cover the needs of the city. Twenty-four-hour crisis lines, food for the hungry, teaching in neighborhood blocks—all are part of the active scene. If only there were enough Watchmen for the *whole* world.

Sunday school children in their classes join to create circles of learning, displaying pride in their pictures by proudly holding up the Bible verses they have memorized. Easter egg hunts are portrayed in the colors of spring from an artist's very bright palette. The end result—kids kneeling on a football field—reminds visitors to this make-believe gallery that everything is *for the glory of the Lord.*

As curator his pride is found only in the pictures and pieces of memorabilia that give glory to his Boss—the Creator and Owner—God. He was called and employed to keep the focus of this gallery clear. As a visionary he constantly searches for more priceless portraits to fill in the empty spaces. There is always room for more.

He personally is featured in only a small "pastoral setting," surrounded by trees and sheep, symbolizing his vast flock. The overhead light is not shining on the curator. It focuses on the Master Shepherd—who is and always will be preeminent in this man's life.

Matted in the colors of the French flag are pictured memories of the summer of 1989, when sixteen hundred French people received Jesus Christ in the morning service. Foreign flavor is captured in these unforgettable scenes as a reminder that language is no barrier to the Holy Spirit and the field is truly the world. Some may caption these scenes as the ultimate altar call. Yet in this sacred gallery, each individual who has met the Lord deems their experience life's ultimate moment. This section is a reminder to pray for those overseas that the fruit will remain and increase.

Continuing through the gallery there is a room for letters and documents that have brought their own art form of gratitude and thanks. Three modestly framed documents display honorary degrees, and the story behind each one is important. His first honorary degree came from Oral Roberts University. The story goes back years ago, when Oral was planning on conducting a citywide event in Kansas City. Many pastors in that area were determined that Oral should never be allowed in Kansas City. They were against his kind of evangelism—a healing ministry, in their eyes, could not be valid. During strong confrontations between local clergy and Oral Roberts, a man came to the front and placed himself between the healing evangelist and the irate ministers. He calmed the crowd, and the tent meeting was allowed. That man who brought his own kind of healing to a sick situation was Tommy Barnett's father.

One day Oral Roberts saw the younger Barnett on television, and was touched with his message of the New Testament church. He called him for an interview. Subsequently, Pastor Barnett became a Regent at the university. When Tommy was given the university honor, the story of Hershel Barnett was told. That degree really belonged to a father and is symbolic of blessings that visit many generations.

The second honorary degree is another example of a father-and-son blessing, and is from Southern California Theological Seminary. The president, Dr. Richard Tucker, was brought up with a twin brother in an agricultural area of Turner, Kansas. His family was poor. The little twin boys were spotted by Hershel Barnett as he was driving by the fields one day. He invited them to his church. They were among twenty children he had packed into his old Dodge car that Sunday. Fortunately he soon purchased a bus! Richard Tucker and his twin brother both rode that bus and found Jesus Christ. Both are in the ministry today.

Another honorary degree that was truly a family affair came from Southwestern College in Waxahachie, Texas. When the school was in Enid, Oklahoma, Pastor Barnett's dad had attended there and met a special young girl named Joy. The school had strong restrictions. There was to be no dating. Both took music lessons from the same teacher, who had a way of not showing up. Their romance was encouraged. A measles epidemic hit the school, and everyone was sent home. Joy wrote a letter to Hershel, which she ended with Psalm 37:4, "Delight thyself also in the Lord; and He shall give thee the desires of thine heart." As a result of that verse they were married before returning to school. There was a rule students could not get married—however, they were allowed to stay, and the product of that verse and marriage was Tommy Barnett.

Moving toward the end of the gallery panorama is a section for the "old masters." Here are treasures from yesteryear. One is a portrait of my dad, captioned "The glory of children are their fathers" (Prov. 17:6).

Another piece, weathered with time, yet as contemporary as this church's ministry, is a word picture of love written by Saint Augustine, who came to faith through the preaching of Bishop Ambrose. Framed to survive the ages for the glory of God, it describes what love looks like.

> It has hands to help others.
> It has feet to hasten to the poor and needy.
> It has eyes to see misery and want.
> It has ears to hear the sighs and sorrows of mankind.
> That is what love looks like.
> —Saint Augustine (354–430)

Master's Commission members are guides in this gallery. They have been preparing their own masterpieces in the months and years gone by. Christ, with His divine brushstrokes, has taken the canvas of these lives and left them with a desire to help others be touched and re-touched by *the* Master Artist.

Toward the end of the gallery is a book whose pages portray visions of current exhibits. More will be added daily and in the years ahead. Always *for the glory of God!*

A true worshiping and working center, not just an imaginary gallery, is open daily at 13613 North Cave Creek Road, Phoenix, Arizona. The public is always welcome!

Ministry Index

MORE PORTRAITS of vision from Phoenix First Assembly are listed in this index. We hope this list of ministries will increase your desire and vision to become a unique and growing center of God's love. The staff of Phoenix First Assembly are eager and willing to assist those of all denominations who would be participants in life's great calling:

Winning souls
Meeting needs
Healing hurts

Aids Ministry
Athletes International Ministries
Audio
Audit
Bernie Cull Street Evangelism
Boys and Girls Missionary
   Crusade
Board of Directors
Bookstore
Bookstore Helpers
Bus Ministry
Bus Mechanics
Businessmen's Breakfast
Celebration Productions
Children's Choir

Children's Church
   For church-attending parents
   For bus children
Choir
Church on the Street
Clown Ministry
Coffee Break
Coffee House Ministry
College and Career
College Campus Ministry
Creative Media Productions
Crusaders for Christ (Singles)
Custodians
Deaf Ministry
Door Greeters

Drama Teams
Epic (Executive Planning and
  Information Committee)
Early Childhood Ministries
Fashion Share Luncheons
Fire Institute (Youth
  Discipleship)
Grooming Ministry
Groundskeepers
Heirborne
His Sheltering Wing
Home Openers
Hospital Visitation
Hurting Parents Ministries
Illustrated Sermons
In Touch (A Housing Network)
Junior Bible Quiz
Junior High Campus Ministry
M.L. Harris Drug and Alcohol
  Awareness Program
Maps (Mobilization and
  Placement)
Master's Commission
Mission Church Builders
Missionettes
Missions
Missions Board
Mormons Ministry
Music Ministry
Nursing Home Ministry
Nursing Home Visitation
Offering Counters
Orchestra
Outdoor Service Ministry
Outreach to Inner City Youth
Overcomers (Alcohol, drug, or
  any chemical dependency)
Park Ministry

Pastoral Care
Pastors School
Political Action Group
Prayer and Crisis Hotline
Preschool Children's Church
Print Shop/Graphic Arts
Prison Ministry
Refiners Institute
Royal Rangers
Saturday Soulwinning Society
Security and Traffic Control
Senior Adults Ministry
Senior High Campus Ministry
Son-Beams (Educably
  handicapped)
Speed the Light
Street Ministry
Sunday School
Sunday School Guides/Greeters
Ushers
Vacation Bible School
Video
Volunteer Pastors
Watchman Ministries
Wednesday Morning
  Intercessory Prayer Group
Wheelchair Buses
Wheelchair Ministry
Wills and Trusts Ministries
Women Counseling Women
Women's Ministry
Young Marrieds
Youth Bible Study
Youth Choir
Youth Detention Home
  Ministry
Youth Ministry
Youth Missions Outreach

About the Author

Tommy Barnett represents a fourth generation of ministry true to traditional Christianity and yet traveling toward the twenty-first century. He manifests himself as innovative, driven, and the architect of a bold spirit of excitement emerging in the church today.

He has authored several books and speaks and appears on television, radio, and to audiences across the continents. His annual pastors' and athletes' conferences, combined with unique and professional holiday events, bring mega-thousands together at Phoenix First Assembly in Phoenix, Arizona. Upwards to fifty thousand have been ministered to in one weekend on the extensive church campus.

In the summer of 1989, sixteen thousand people visiting from France came to faith during a Sunday morning altar call—historic in itself. A result of this pastor's goal to win souls, heal hurts, and meet needs.

As a young evangelist he traveled the world with record crowds for that era. His first church in Davenport, Iowa, became the fastest growing church in America. That honor repeated itself in the Phoenix church whose growth has been legendary.

Often described as a "distance runner" he continues his dedicated marathon to take the life-changing message of Jesus Christ to mankind, leaving footprints of faith, love, trust, hope, and vision to those who follow.

If you or someone you know would like to attend the annual Pastors' Conference, please write to:

Tommy Barnett's Pastors' School
Phoenix First Assembly
13613 North Cave Creek Road
Phoenix, AZ 85022